BRISTOL RECORD SOCIETY'S
PUBLICATIONS

General Editor: JOSEPH BETTEY, M.A., Ph.D., F.S.A.
Assistant Editor: MISS ELIZABETH RALPH, M.A., F.S.A.

VOL. XLIV

TUDOR WILLS PROVED IN BRISTOL

1546–1603

TUDOR WILLS PROVED IN BRISTOL
1546–1603

EDITED BY
SHEILA LANG & MARGARET McGREGOR

Printed for the
BRISTOL RECORD SOCIETY
1993

ISBN 0 901538 14 0
ISSN 0305 8730

Bristol Record Society is grateful to Miss Elizabeth Ralph and to the Marc Fitch Fund for grants in support of this volume.

Produced for the Society by
Alan Sutton Publishing Limited, Stroud, Glos
Printed in Great Britain

CONTENTS

ACKNOWLEDGEMENTS

We should like to thank John Williams the City Archivist and our colleagues at Bristol Record Office for their help, particularly Anne Bradley for assistance with the biographical research and also our families especially David, James and Malcolm McGregor and Kate, George and Andrew Lang for their word processing skills together with Edwin George who assisted with the glossary.

EDITORIAL NOTE

The general principles followed are mentioned in the introduction. Where it has been desired to record original spellings these have been placed in ( ) after the modern version. Editorial additions are shown in [ ] while editorial comments are in italics. A few of the wills are in poor condition and missing sections are indicated thus: ——.

LIST OF ABBREVIATIONS

admon. administration
als.   alias
appr.   apprentice(s)/apprenticed
B.R.O. Bristol Record Office
bur.   bur.
burg.   burgess

County names:

Berks.	Berkshire	Herefs.	Herefordshire	Salop.	Shropshire
Cambs.	Cambridgeshire	Mons.	Monmouthshire	Som.	Somerset
Carm.	Carmartheshire	Oxon.	Oxfordshire	Wilts.	Wiltshire
Gloucs.	Gloucestershire	Pembs.	Pembrokeshire	Worcs.	Worcestershire

d.o.   daughter of
decd.   deceased
husb.   husbandman
m.   married
P.C.C. Prerogative Court of Canterbury

Personal names [abbreviated in index only]:

Ag.	Agnes	Eliz.	Elizabeth	Mich.	Michael
Alex.	Alexander	Elnr.	Eleanor	Nath.	Nathaniel
Andr.	Andrew	Flor.	Florence	Nich.	Nicholas
Ann	Anne	Geo.	George	Phil.	Philip
Anth.	Anthony	Hen.	Henry	Rich.	Richard
Arth.	Arthur	Humph.	Humphrey	Robt.	Robert
Barth.	Bartholomew	Jas.	James	Rog.	Roger
Chas.	Charles	Kath.	Katherine	Rowl.	Rowland
Chris.	Christopher	Laur.	Laurence	Sam.	Samuel
Cic.	Cicely	Leon.	Leonard	Sim.	Simon
Dan.	Daniel	Margt.	Margaret	Theo.	Theophilus
Dor.	Dorothy	Margy.	Margery	Thos.	Thomas
Edm.	Edmund	Maur.	Maurice	Walt.	Walter
Edw.	Edward	Math.	Mathew	Wm.	William

s.o.   son of
S.T.C. Short Title Catalogue
wf.   wife
wid.   widow

INTRODUCTION

During the years 1972 to 1978 members of a class organised by Bristol University Extra-Mural Department to study archives in the keeping of Bristol Record Office devoted their attention to transcribing the earliest wills found in the probate records originating from the Diocese of Bristol. These transcripts were issued, *in extenso*, as two booklets in duplicated form in 1975 and 1978. The plan was to continue the transcriptions to the end of Elizabeth's reign, covering 368 wills in all. The work of transcription continued although the production of further booklets was not possible. In due course it seemed desirable to bring the material so transcribed to a wider audience through publication.

The quantity of material involved was too great for all the wills to be published as transcripts. It was therefore decided to include only the wills of testators resident in the city or its suburbs (thus omitting wills relating to the rural parishes to the north and west of the city which were in the archdeaconry) and to calendar the chosen wills thus rendering them both briefer and more readily comprehensible. Nothing of any substance has been omitted from the chosen wills and every personal name is given. Although spelling has otherwise been modernised, numerous brief quotations are given exactly as they occur in the wills and the exact spelling is given for obsolete words and also for surnames. The will numbered 105 in this present volume is the last to be included in the booklets referred to above. Up to and including no. 105 the calendars have been prepared direct from the booklets although any errors which came to light were, of course, rectified. Later wills were calendared from the class transcripts which were checked against the original wills. Each of the two booklets was issued with an introduction by the late Professor Patrick McGrath and the former City Archivist, Miss Mary E. Williams. The present editors are greatly indebted to their work which is largely incorporated in the introductory comments which follow, although some amendment and extension has been necessary to accommodate the omission of the earlier "country" wills and the inclusion of later material. We should also like to record our thanks to the various members of the Archives Class over the years, whose labours provided the basis for this present volume.

The wills in this archive group were proved in the Consistory Court of Bristol, which was held in Bristol Cathedral. They remained in the care of the Court until 1858 when they were transferred to the District Probate Registry. In 1958, they were transferred to the Bristol Record Office.

The earliest surviving will in this group is dated 1546 and is that of Richard Fetchett, who had been one of the brethren of the College of St. Mark in Bristol. After that there is a gap until 1568. Of the 192 surviving Bristol city wills for the period 1546 to March 1602/3, an unbroken series appears only from 1597 (wills 53 to 186) although 29 wills survive for 1593 and 14 for 1574; the survival of half-a-dozen city wills for 1559 (nos. 187–192) is discussed below. It is clear that only a small part of the total number of wills which must have been made during these years has survived. Amongst Bristol's civic records is the Great Orphan Book in which copies of some wills were registered. During the years 1546–1593, for example, 147 wills were registered in these books, 22 of which were proved either in the Prerogative Court of Canterbury or the Probate Court of the Bishop of London, but there seems to be no satisfactory explanation as to why the remainder are not found among the wills of Bristol Consistory Court.

A collection of 10 wills dated 1559 was found some years ago among the capitular records of the Dean and Chapter but no copies of these are to be found in the records of Bristol Consistory Court. These were published in the Transactions of the Bristol and Gloucester Archaeological Society in 1943; the ones relating to the city are included at the end of the present volume in an appendix.

The wills surviving in the group are therefore clearly only a part of the total number which must have been made. It has been suggested that some of the Consistory Court records were destroyed in the Bristol Riots of 1831 when rioters broke into the Chapter House where the court records were stored. However, all the gaps in the series cannot be explained in this way for in 1830 the House of Commons required a return of wills in the various Probate Registries. The return for Bristol gave the earliest will as 1568 and the next as 1571 but said that from 1571 the series appeared to be regularly registered. In reality there are only 3 wills for 1571 and thereafter some years are missing. Presumably the person making the return thumbed hastily through the collection and reported regular registration from 1571. In fact the earliest surviving will in the group is now known to be dated 1546; this will was known to Bishop Secker who *c*.1735 mentioned it in connection with the dedication of Clifton parish church [see Bristol Record Society's Publications vol. XXXVII].

Although it does not survive, the wills were in fact entered into a register. Some of the wills from 1593 onwards have register folio numbers noted on them; the earliest noted is folio 318 so many earlier wills must have been registered. The wills are, for the most part, endorsed with the year of registration; although this normally corresponds with the date of probate there can be discrepancies, for example the will of Alice Batten was made in May 1591 and administration was granted in August of that year yet the endorsement was 1593. The present arrangement is by years of probate as endorsed (old style years, hence running from 25 March to 24 March the following year) and within such years, in alphabetical order. It must be understood therefore that prior to 1593 the wills printed here form a random group which has happened to survive and is not a complete collection of Elizabethan wills proved at Bristol. It must also be remembered that the "more substantial" citizens are likely to have had their wills proved in the higher court, the Prerogative Court of Canterbury, so at best we are dealing here with persons of more modest means. From this group of wills alone it would be dangerous to make any generalisations about all the inhabitants of Elizabethan Bristol, although some general statements can be made. As the wills have survived in greater numbers for the later part of Elizabeth's reign a more general picture can be gained for that period. It is unfortunate that these wills cannot be supplemented by probate inventories; one or two wills have the total value of the inventory noted on the bottom but the inventories have not survived in these cases. Only four of Bristol's probate inventories are of Tudor date and none relates to a surviving will.

Of the 192 wills included in this volume, 145 are of men and 47 of women, most but not all of whom were widows. Not every will named the testator's parish nor could it always be deduced from the desired place of burial, but of those for which a parish could be named, St. Stephen was represented by 21 wills and St. Thomas by 19 while St. Peter and St. Philip each had 17. St. Mary Redcliffe had 15 and Temple and Christchurch each 14. There were a dozen wills for St. James and 9 for St. Nicholas, 5 each for St. Michael and St. Augustine, 4 for Barton Hundred, 3 for St. Mary le Port and 2 each for the remaining parishes except St. Mark's for which there was one, unless one were also to count Cicely Lady Berkeley,who stated no parish, desired burial in the Cathedral but resided at the Gaunts.

Well over 50 different occupations are represented amongst the testators, although many appear once only, for example: collier, musician, gunner, furber, cook, lighterman, trumpeter, petty chapman and surgeon. The most frequently recurring trade is that of tailor, with 10 examples whilst several shearmen and several tanners also appear and clergy too are well represented. Some occupations are most likely to occur in certain parishes; yeomen are to be found in St. James or St. Philip whereas the cloth trade is clearly centred on Temple.

The wills here transcribed vary greatly in the amount of information given and the light they throw on 16th century Bristol. Collectively they tell us a great deal and it is worthwhile drawing attention to some which are of particular interest.

The first will is that of Richard Fetchett, a priest in St. Mark's Hospital, who made his will in 1546, the thirty-eighth year of Henry VIII "defendor of the faithe and of the churche of englande and also of Irlonde in earth supreame hedd". Richard made numerous bequests of vestments, altar cloths and surplices. He expected his beneficiaries to pray for his soul and made arrangements for memorial services. The changing religious background of the mid-sixteenth century is reflected in the second will in which Agnes Saunders in 1568 commends her soul to God "trustinge to be saved only by the Deathe and passion of our savioure Jeseus christ".

There are many references in the wills to clothing and household furnishings, particularly beds. Catherine Fesaunt widow, for example, in 1593 (no. 45) left her servant "one flocke bed, one bolster of fethers, one paire of sheetes iii Ruges for a bed, one Ketle, a petticoate with Mocadoe bodies . . .". Edith Mason (no. 178) seems to have owned a sizeable wardrobe for she was able to bequeath to her daughters some 5 aprons, her best petticoat, 5 smocks and 9 kerchiefs together with other items including a stamell waiscoat. Thomas Flemynge in 1602 must have cut a fine figure in his seal skin jerkin and buff breeches with silver lace (no. 156). Thomas Barwell, a clothworker of Temple, made a will (no. 166) which reads almost like an inventory; timber for improvements to his house was being stored with his neighbours and there were 10 windows and 20 doors awaiting use. The greatest affluence is probably shown by Cicely, Lady Berkeley, who left a gold chain and cross, a flower of diamonds and a basin and ewer of silver,parcel gilt, displaying the Berkeley arms (no. 187).

A small number of wills throw light on trade. A weaver of St. Thomas (William Turner, no. 20) left his son four looms "with all thinges that dothe belong unto them"; his wife was to hand them over to his son at age 24 having been "made as good in all poyntes as they were at the day of my buryall". Thomas Collins, a freemason, (no. 30), left quantities of Bath stone and Dundry stone, "all my chimneys", old lead and solder, "all my best Axes with one dozen and a half of tooles", various other implements, "my penne & Inkhorne with all my drawinge tooles" and "my bookes of byldynge . . . . with my draught plottes". A blacksmith in St. Peter's left his son the great anvil in the shop which apparently the son was already using (no. 140). A hooper's widow left "Coopers Tymber Twigges hoopes and vessells of Tymber wrought & unwrought". The will of Edmund Auflitt, chandler, left his furnace to his son (no. 133) whilst a baker, Thomas Masson, refers to an investment of £30 in his business made by his nephew (no. 122). An indication of the time taken in manufacture is given by a clothworker of Temple (no. 134) who in 1600 left his brother "two fyne graye Cottons" to raise money to satisfy bequests of £6. There was a proviso that if the brother did not like the cottons ready made at the testator's decease he was to wait 7 weeks or two months until the testator's widow could make some to his liking.

One or two of the wills refer to craft organisations in Bristol. Cicely Nayler, widow, made various bequests to her apprentice and forgave him "his covennante yeare which he hathe to serve with all his benefitt and profitt of that yeare"; she also added "I do give and bequeathe to the mystery and companye of the whoopers xs to drinke the day of my funerall"(no. 70). Elizabeth Williams, widow, of St. Peter's, requested that "iiij men that have bine wardens of the companie of the pointemakers to carrye me to the church (and) lay me in the grave". For this, she left 6s (no. 83). Nicholas Woulfe, a joiner, left his company 3s 4d "to drinke after mye buriall" (no. 148).

One or two of the testators showed a concern for education. Francis Dennys, gentleman of St. Philip's, wanted his godson to be apprenticed at the age of 16 but added "I hope that such as shall have that smale stocke in their hands will keepe the boy at scoole at least wyse to write reade & cast Accompt . . ." (no. 35). Daniel White, a mariner of St. Nicholas, in 1598 instructed his wife "that shee shall bringe up my children to their Learninge" (no. 129) whilst a year previously Thomas Rogers of Temple had instructed that his son Edward be brought up to school and to learning until he was able to be put to some occupation (no. 76).

Most references to books were in the wills of clerics. Thomas Rider, clerk, of Redcliffe, left his son "all my boockes" (no. 75) and William Jacy, parson of St.Michael's,bequeathed "all my books and my lute" (no. 97). Richard Fetchett in 1546 left 5 volumes of "the whole workes of Vyncent". By far the most detailed was the will of John Knight, Vicar of All Saints (no. 68). His collection included Martinius's Hebrew Grammar, "Daneus upon the small Prophetts", Henry Smith's Sermons, Piscator's works and Fox's Prayers. His "great studie bible" was given to his wife whilst the residue of his books was bequeathed to two preachers of the word of God.

Although many Elizabethans kept weapons in their houses for self-defence and for use in time of national emergency relatively few of these testators specifically refer to them. John Knight, mentioned above, bequeathed a dagger knife and a crooked sword and Thomas Rider left a bow and arrows as did Hugh Cecill, a carpenter (no. 56). Richard White, a merchant (no. 192) in leaving his share of a ship in 1559, included ordnance and munitions in the bequest. Hugh Harvye, a scrivener (no. 94), left a petronel with flask and touchbox.

National events scarcely figure in these wills so it is particularly interesting to find in 1598, the year when there was a major Irish rebellion against Elizabeth I, the will of Theophilus Fletcher, gentleman of Bristol,late of the city of London, who stated he was "now bound for Irelande and fully determined to serve her majestie in her warres there". Very charmingly he left to his sister Priscilla £5 "to be bestowed upon some prittie jewell, the which I praie her to kepe and to weare for my sake" (no. 90).

Taken as a whole the wills provide some useful information about the economic and social life of Elizabethan Bristol, showing the property interests of the testators, the goods in their houses and the money they owed or had owing to them. Some indication of the cost of living is given by a shearman who required his brother to maintain his wife "with sufficient maintaynance for a woman of her degree or els payinge her yerly . . . v li at her choyce" (no. 95). Unfortunately we do not know the value of the goods "moveable and unmoveable" which Joan Burnett, a cardmaker's widow, left to William Edwards, cardmaker, on condition that he "shall tende and find mee meate and drinke and all thinges necessary during my lief" as well as to bury her and pay the funeral expenses (no. 87). Elizabeth Bantonn in 1599 owed her servant Bess Cutler 9s for three quarters' wages although some clothing had been given in part-payment (no. 107).

Twenty-three of the wills were nuncupative or spoken. By their very nature these tend to be brief but their particular interest lies in the reporting of the actual words spoken. Harry May, in 1573 (no. 8) began: "I knowe I shall nowe dye and not recover and there is but one way with me" whilst a young apprentice, Melchisedich Androwes in 1601 had the audacity, *in extremis*, to speak thus to his mistress: "yow have no nede of anie thinge that I have, For yow are ritche ynoughe" (no. 150). The briefest will ever must be that of the widow Annes Masone who, on being asked whom she would make executor, "straygte way put her hand forth and tooke her Cosen Ann Clovyll by the hand and sayd ann and therewith all held her faste" (no. 121).

Despite the formal wording of most of the other wills, the individual personalities of the testators can be glimpsed on occasion. James Johnes, a shearman of Temple, arranged for his wife to remain in his house (keeping his children at her own expense) for 6 months after which she was to receive a lump sum £15. She was then permitted to lease the house if she could agree a rate with the executor, if not "she is to have her money and so departe" (no. 158). By contrast a joiner of St. Leonard's (no. 163) declared in 1602: "I am but a poore man and all the goodes and chattles that I have I give and bequeathe unto Dorothie my wiffe and wold soe doe yf I had ten tymes as muche".

Less than half the testators make any bequest to the poor and such bequests as are made are not remarkably munificent: 10s to each of two parishes to be distributed in bread (no. 58) is perhaps typical of the more generous testators whilst the less generous might give 3s 4d, as Elizabeth Dole did to the poor men's box of St. Peter's in 1571 (no. 3). Roger Cook's gift of £5 "to the hospitall" is outstanding (no. 57) whilst the poorest prisoners in Newgate were doubtless grateful for the 6s 8d they received from Thomas Dole in 1597 (no. 61). Cicely Lady Berkeley in 1559 required her executors "to do dedes of charitie for my soule and Christen soules to the pleasure of allmightie god" (no. 187). The most enduring charitable donation was made by John Winchombe, a yeoman, who left to the poor of St. Philip's "dwelling in the Hundreade" a heifer, believed to be with calf; when, in due course, the heifer should "waxe old" she was to be replaced "and so for evermore to contynue" (no. 131).

Small monetary gifts to the clergy are occasionally recorded, thus Robert Burges gave 3s 4d to the minister of St. Thomas's (no. 85) and Richard Cooper, clothier, left 5s to the vicar of Temple parish, although this may be payment for writing the will (no. 88). John Hope, vintner, bequeathed 40s to the vicar of St. Nicholas and 10s to Mr. Arthur, parson of St. Mary le Port as well as 5s to the parish clerk (no. 96). James Taylor left 5s to the vicar of Temple who had written the will (no. 128) who also received 10s from another testator,Thomas Beese (no. 134). It is clear that many of the wills were in fact drawn up by members of the clergy. Christopher Deveroux, curate of St. Peter's, is stated to have drawn up will no. 3 and received 3s 4d for his pains. Wills number 9, 14 and 20 are written in the same hand, which is probably that of the clerk of St. Mary Redcliffe.

In the light of the above, it is questionable to what degree the expressions of religious belief, which appear in virtually every will, represent the views of the testator. The religious upheavals of the time are reflected in the strong contrast between the will of Richard Fetchett, priest, of 1546 who repeatedly asked prayers for his soul and who left money for masses, or David Harte who in 1559 left his soul to God and "to our blessed Ladye Sainte Marye and to all the hollye companye of heavin" and later testators who trusted to be saved only by the death and passion of Jesus Christ or whose wills included some form of words indicating a Protestant, even Calvinistic, commitment, as in the case of Margaret Chaundler who died in 1601 or 1602 "trustinge to arise at the Laste day, when the Trumpe shall Blowe and then through thy greate mercie to inherite a place in the Kingdome of Heaven which thou haste prepared for thine Electe from the Begininge" (no. 169).

A couple of wills hint at a fashion for extravagant funerals which had become common during the later sixteenth century: Francis Dennys, a gentleman, wished to be buried "as my neihbors ar buryed & no otherwyse" (no. 35) whilst another gentleman, Patrick White, of Temple, wished to be laid in some convenient place without any pomp "ore extraordinarie Chardge" (no. 145). More humble citizens aspired to burial in their chosen spot ("as nighe my mother as may be", "amongst my other bretherne and Sisterne" or "as neare unto my pewe doore as maye be" (nos. 89, 3, 74) with sometimes a few shillings allowed for drinking on the day of the funeral (no. 83).

Some of the expressions of religious faith expressed may indeed have been purely conventional but in many cases the words exceed the conventional expectations and appear to come from the heart. Daniel White, a mariner, instructed his wife concerning his children, that she "be carefull of their bringinge up in the feare of God" (no. 129). John Gibson looked forward to the time when his "soul and bodie shall bee reunited togeather and enioy the kingdome of heaven" (no. 173) while George Laurence, clerk of the parish of All Saints, expressed his faith in the forgiveness of sins through the "meere mercye" of God, Who would make him "inheritour with him of the everlastinge ioyes in heaven . . . And this I end upon Thursday beinge the eightenth day of October & the xxxv th yeare of the raigne of owr Sovereine and vertuous Queene Elizabeth".

LIST OF WILLS

1.	1546	FECHETT, RICHARD	priest	[St. Mark]
2.	1568	SAWNDERS, AGNES	widow	St. Augustine
3.	1570	DOLE, ELIZABETH	widow	St. Peter
4.	1571	COSTON, FRANCIS		St. Nicholas
5.	1571	APOWELL, EDWARD	victualler	St. Nicholas
6.	1571	POWELL, CHRISTOPHER		Bristol
7.	1571	STONE, WILLIAM		Temple
8.	1573	MAY, HARRY		St. Nicholas
9.	1574	BECK, JOAN	widow	St. Mary Redcliffe
10.	1574	COMPANE alias FYANNE, JANE	widow	St. Stephen
11.	1574	EDWARDS, WILLIAM	farrier	[St. Michael]
12.	1574	HERBERT, SIMON	brewer	[St. Michael]
13.	1574	HYLL, ALAN	merchant	[St. Stephen]
14.	1574	HOPKYN, WILLIAM		St. Mary Redcliffe
15.	1574	HUNT, GEORGE	whittawer	[St. James]
16.	1574/5	LEWIS/LEUES, AGNES	widow	Christchurch
17.	1574	LEWIS, JOHN	pointmaker	Christchurch
18.	1574/5	NEWMAN, RICHARD	butcher	St. Nicholas
19.	1574	NORTHALL, ROLAND		St. Mary Redcliffe
20.	1574	TURNER, WILLIAM	weaver	St. Thomas
21.	1574	WAWEN, EDWARD		St. Mary Redcliffe
22.	1574	YEMAN, WILLIAM	glover	Bristol
23.	1592/3	DAVIS, MORGAN	wireworker	St. Mary Redcliffe
24.	1593	ANDROWS, AGNES	widow	Bristol
25.	1593	BARNES, DAVID	tucker	Temple
26.	1593	BATTEN, ALICE		St. Werburgh
27.	1593	BEYMAND, HARRY	dyer	St. James
28.	1593	CAROWE, DARBYE	petty chapman	St. Mary Redcliffe
29.	1593	CLERKE, RICHARD	pointmaker	St. James
30.	1593/4	COLLINS, THOMAS	freemason	St. Philip & London
31.	1593	COLWAYE, OWEN	surgeon	St. Stephen
32.	1593	DALLOWE, THOMAS	tailor	St. John
33.	1593	DAVIS, LEWIS		St. Philip
34.	1593/4	DAVIS, THOMAS	hooper	St. Stephen
35.	1593	DENNYS, FRANCIS	gent.	Barton Hundred
36.	1593	ELLIOT, CHRISTIAN	widow	St. Philip
37.	1593	FORD, HELEN	widow	St. Nicholas
38.	1593	FREELYNGE, ANNE	widow	St. Peter
39.	1593/4	GOODYERE, ANTHONY	tailor	Bristol
40.	1593	JAMES, JOHN	tailor	St. Stephen
41.	1593	JONES, THOMAS		St. Thomas

42. 1593	LACYE, JONAS	clerk	Bristol
43. 1593	LAURENCE, GEORGE	clerk	St. Stephen
44. 1593/4	A PENDRYE, GILLIAN	widow	St. Thomas
45. 1593/4	FESAUNT, KATHERINE	widow	[St. Stephen]
46. 1593	RISBY, ROBERT		Barton Hundred
47. 1593	ROBYNS, NICHOLAS	tailor	St. Mary le Port
48. 1593	ROGERS, THOMAS	tanner	St. Mary Redcliffe
49. 1593	SCULLICK, ELIZABETH	widow	St. Augustine
50. 1593/4	SHORE, RICHARD	yeoman	St. James
51. 1593	TAWNYE, JOHN	bowyer	Christchurch
52. 1593	WILLIAMS, RICHARD		St. Philip
53. 1597/8	BAYLIE alias PITTS, AGNES		Bristol
54. 1597	BAYLYE, NICHOLAS	trumpeter	St. Stephen
55. 1597	BOYDELL, WILLIAM	merchant	[Christchurch]
56. 1597	CICILL, HUGH	carpenter	St. Philip
57. 1597	COOK, ROGER	tanner	[St. Philip]
58. 1597	CORNISH, RALPH	tailor	Christchurch
59. 1597	COULTON, JOHN	whittawer	[?St. James]
60. 1597	COULTON, KATHERINE	widow	St. James
61. 1597	DOLE, THOMAS	yeoman	[St. Peter]
62. 1597	FREWELL, ROBERT		Bristol
63. 1597	HANBYE, WILLIAM	freemason	St. Philip
64. 1597	HULL alias HILL, MAURICE		St. Philip
65. 1597	HUNT, JOHN	tanner	[St. Peter]
66. 1597	JONES, ELIZABETH	widow	St. Mary Redcliffe
67. 1597	JOONS, MARGARET	widow	[St. Thomas]
68. 1597	KNIGHT, JOHN	vicar	All Saints
69. 1597/8	MOWREY, THOMAS	tailor	St. Nicholas
70. 1597	NAYLER, CICELY	widow	St. Stephen
71. 1597	NICHOLLS, EDWARD		St. Thomas
72. 1597	OLFYLDE, MARY	singlewoman	Christchurch
73. 1597	POPLEY, EDMUND	ironmonger	[Christchurch]
74. 1597	POWELL, JOHN	shoemaker	St. Peter
75. 1597	RIDER, THOMAS	clerk	Redcliffe
76. 1597	ROGERS/REGERES, THOMAS		Temple
77. 1597	SYMONS, JOAN	widow	St. Ewen
78. 1597	VEYSEY, JOHN	tailor	St. Peter
79. 1597	VINCENT, JOHN		St. Thomas
80. 1597	WAKER, ELIZABETH	widow	St. Mary le Port
81. 1597	WESTACOTT, RICHARD	mariner	Bristol
82. 1597	WHITEHEAD, PETER	yeoman	St. Philip
83. 1597	WILLIAMS, ELIZABETH	widow	St. Peter
84. 1597	YOUNGE, MARGARET	widow	Christchurch
85. 1598/9	BURGES, ROBERT	butcher	St. Thomas
86. 1598	BURGES, SAMPSON		Redcliffe
87. 1598	BURNETT, JOAN	widow	Bristol
88. 1598	COOPER, RICHARD	clothier	Temple
89. 1598	EDWARDS, EDMOND	baker	St. Thomas
90. 1598	FLETCHER, THEOPHILUS	gent.	Bristol (late London)
91. 1598	GARRETT, ROBERT		St. Peter
92. 1598	GOODMAN, THOMAS		Bristol
93. 1598	GOSNELL, JULIAN	widow	St. Ewen
94. 1598	HARVYE, HUGH	scrivener	St. Peter
95. 1598/9	HAYWARD, THOMAS	shearman	Bristol
96. 1598	HOPE, JOHN	vintner	Bristol
97. 1598	JACY, WILLIAM	clerk	St. Michael
98. 1598	LEY, JOHN		St. John the Baptist
99. 1598	LONG, MAURICE	Bristol	

100.	1598/9	MANNINGE, RICHARD	pewterer	Barton Hundred
101.	1598	SAUNDERS, WILLIAM	sailor	St. Stephen
102.	1598	SETTLE, THOMAS	turner	St. Stephen
103.	1598	SMITH, RICHARD	shearman	Temple
104.	1598/9	WOODNEY, WILLIAM		[St. James]
105.	1597/8	WRIGHT, MARGERY	widow	St. Thomas
106.	1599	APPRICE, ALICE	widow	St. Philip
107.	1599	BANTONN, ELIZABETH	widow	St.Thomas
108.	1599	BELCHER, TOBY	merchant	St. Peter
109.	1599	BUTLER, WILLIAM	tailor	St. Philip and Jacob
110.	1599	CHAMBERS, ALICE	singlewoman	Christchurch
111.	1599	COOCKE, JOHN	weaver	St. Mary Redcliffe
112.	1599/ 1600	CORYE, ROBERT	husbandman	St. Philip
113.	1599/ 1600	DURAND, MORRIS	minister	St. Werburgh
114.	1599	FORD, AGNES	singlewoman	Christchurch
115.	1599	GLEWE, RICHARD		St. Stephen
116.	1599	GREGE, THOMAS		
117.	1599	JONES, DAVID		St. Nicholas
118.	1599	JONSON, EDITH	widow	St. James
119.	1599	LANGTON, MARGARET	widow	St. Peter
120.	1599	MARTEN, AGNES	[widow]	St. Mary le Port
121.	1599	MASONE, AGNES	widow	[?St. Stephen]
122.	1599	MASSON, THOMAS	baker	[St. Stephen]
123.	1599/ 1600	NEWTONN, JAMES		St. Thomas
124.	1599	PACKER, WILLIAM	yeoman	St. James
125.	1599	PANTHURE, ARTHUR		Christchurch
126.	1599	ROTHELL alias ROTHEWELL, JOHN	brewer	[St. James]
127.	1599	SIMONS, ALICE	widow	Christchurch
128.	1599/ 1600	TAYLOR, JAMES	clothworker	Temple
129.	1599	WHITE, DANIEL	mariner	St. Nicholas
130.	1599	WHITTE, JOAN	widow	Bristol
131.	1599	WINCHOMBE, JOHN	yeoman	St. Philip
132.	1600	ADEANE, JOHN	soapmaker	[St. Thomas]
133.	1600	AUFLITT alias ALFLATT, EDMUND	chandler	St. Thomas
134.	1600	BEESE, THOMAS	clothworker	Temple
135.	1600	BROCKE, ROBERT	bachelor	Temple
136.	1600/1	BUSHE, THOMAS	tanner	Bristol
137.	1600/1	BYRDE, JOHN	shearman	Temple
138.	1600	DITTIE, ANTHONY	musician	[St. Thomas]
139.	1600	HENDLYE, ROGER	yeoman	[St. James]
140.	1600	HYLL, THOMAS	blacksmith	St. Peter
141.	1600	MORRICE, NICHOLAS	sailor	St. Michael
142.	1600	NICHOLAS, WILLIAM	tanner	St. Mary Redcliffe
143.	1600	POPE, ROBERT	husbandman	Barton Hundred
144.	1600/1	POYNER, CLEMENCE	widow	All Saints
145.	1600	WHITE, PATRICK	gent.	Temple
146.	1600	WIDGINS/WIGGINS, WILLIAM		St. Peter
147.	1600	WIETT/WYETT/WYATT, SILVESTER		St. Stephen
148.	1600	WOULFE, NICHOLAS	joiner	St. Stephen
149.	1600	YEMAN/YEOMAN, JOHN	grocer	[St. Mary Redcliffe]

150.	1601	ANDROWES, MELCHISEDICH	apprentice	St. Thomas
151.	1601	AVERY, EDWARD	collier	St. Philip
152.	1601	AWSTINE, WILLIAM		Redcliffe
153.	1601/2	BIRKEN, THOMAS	joiner	St. Stephen
154.	1601	BURTTE, WILLIAM	hooper	St. Stephen
155.	1601	DAIES/DEYOS, JOYCE	widow	St. Thomas
156.	1601	FLEMYNGE, THOMAS		[St. Peter]
157.	1601	HAWLE, RICHARD	innkeeper	St. Thomas
158.	1601	JOHNES, JAMES	shearman	Temple
159.	1601	LLOYDE, DAVID JOHN	miller	St. Peter
160.	1601	PITTES, JOHN	preacher	Bristol
161.	1601	READINGE, HUGH	gunner	Bristol
162.	1601	STAPLE, JOHN	furber	Bristol
163.	1601/2	WILLIAMS, DAVID	joiner	St. Leonard
164.	1601	WILSON, EDWARD	sergeant	Christchurch
165.	1602	ALDWORTH, THOMAS	hooper	Bristol
166.	1602	BARWELL, THOMAS	clothworker	Temple
167.	1602/3	BATTIN, JERVIS	cutler	St. Thomas
168.	1602	BONNER, JOAN	widow	Bristol
169.	1602	CHAUNDLER, MARGARET	[married woman]	
170.	1602	CLARKE, JOHN	pointmaker	St. James
171.	1602	CROUCHINGTONN, WILLIAM		St. Thomas
172.	1602	DAVIES, ALICE	widow	St. Stephen
173.	1602	GIBSON, JOHN	cook	
174.	1602	GOODDIAR/GOODYER, JOAN	widow	St. Michael
175.	1602	GRAYE, JOHN	clothier	Temple
176.	1602/3	JONES, MAUD	widow	St. Peter
177.	1602/3	KEMBLE, MARY	widow	St. Augustine
178.	1602	MASON, EDITH	widow	St. Nicholas
179.	1602/3	MAYNE, SIMON	yeoman	St. Philip
180.	1602	PROSSER/PRORSER, RICHARD	tailor	St. Leonard
181.	1602	STONES, JOHN	weaver	St. Philip
182.	1602	SYON, MARGARET	widow	St. Peter
183.	1602	TYPPETT, JOHN	lighterman	St. Augustine
184.	1602	WALLIS, JOHN	labourer	Redcliffe
185.	1602/3	WELSHE, RICHARD	tailor	St. Stephen
186.	1602	WHITE, WILLIAM	mariner	Bristol

APPENDIX

187.	1559	BERKELEY, CICELY	Lady, widow	[St. Augustine]
188.	1559	HARTE, DAVID	burgess	Temple
189.	1559	HARTE, WILLIAM	baker	Christchurch
190.	1559	MERICKE, JOHN		
191.	1559	MORSE. RICHARD	St. Philip	
192.	1559	WHITE, RICHARD	merchant	St. Stephen

INDEX OF TESTATORS

CALENDAR OF
WILLS

1 RICHARD FECHETT, priest, Bristol, 22 August 1546.

Being sick of body; "remembring the mutabilitie and uncertentie of this fraile and —— and moost specyallie the casuall and sudayne —— perethe . And willing therfore to prepare and make myself —— that behalf apperteynethe, make and ordeyne this my pre[sent testament] —— in maner and forme following. And first —— vile world and all the yoyes and del—— commytting my self to almyghtie god my —— grace that I may be particypatt with —— yoye and felicitie, as he hathe prepar[ed]".

To be buried within the "Quyer" of the parish —— St. Mark's church, "And for that place for my grave" 6s 8d. To the said parish church of St. —— otherwise called the Gaunts, a pair of vestments of blue "tyssew", an altar cloth of diaper with a mass book. To sir John Ellis curate of that church 3s 4d in money "and oon of my best Surplices at the discrecion of my executor to be delyvered to hym for a remembraunce to praye for my Soule and all my Frendes and all Christen Sowles".

To sir John Robyns, priest, "my goostlie Father" one of his surplices and a gown of brown blue of the best, a jacket at the discretion of his executor and a doublet of worsted with a pair of "hoses" of the best and 5 books which is the whole works of "Vyncentt" and another book called "Sermones discipuli", a dirige book of vellum with a clasp of silver and gilt. To sir Thomas Pynchyn a bow and 8 arrows —— and glove and 3s 4d in money for a remembrance to pray for his soul.

To the altar of the crowd [crypt] within the parish church of St. John the Baptist in Bristol a pair of green vestments there always to be occupied. To the parish of St. Matthew (Mathos) otherwise called the church of Clifton, Gloucs. a pair of vestments of Bruges satin (brigges satten) with a [?]green orphrey (offras) and 2s in money to that church.

For "a gentle remembrance" Edward Pryn to have delivered to him by executor to keep dirige and mass and to make a drinking to that company of that parish after dirige 5s and —— to remain there. To Edward Pryn a mass [book] of vellum "which he hathe in his keping alredye And [?Mar]garett his [?wife] xs in money for hir gentlenes showed and paynes takyng for me".

To William Tyndall, merchant, "my Jangler otherwise called Klar——" [?clarion]. To John Halydaye one of my saye jackets at the discretion of

1

my executor and my cloak. To William Babbe, Mr. Colman's cook, in money 26s 8d and my garden tools —— other tools in my house and a grind stone and 2 broaches toward ho—— and a chafron to heat water in with an old mortar and pestle to the same and a "bowee" [?bow].

To Thomas Davys late servant to the house of Gaunts and Joan his wife 40s in money and a grey trotting nag with the hay in my Lady "barkleys" stable. To Joan wife of Thomas Cootes 3s and a pair of short "hoses" which I made of late. To Margaret Sprott my old black gown and a shirt with a pair of "hoses". To Welthian Hooper sometime wife of John Towker 20d to pray for my soul. Unto "Fyrme John Awnddes Son of Clyfton" an old jacket to make him a coat. To Richard, Edward Pryn's servant, a jacket. To Thomas Awndd son of John Awndd my short old gown. To sir John Bradley a pair of —— to pray for me. To David Hillyns wife a "bedes" ——. To Maurice (Morys) Baten's wife a pair of beads (bedes). To Philip Williams and —— and a carpet for a table for ——. To Edwa[rd] Colte ——. To sir John —— my master to pray for me 20s.

To the reparations of highways at discretion of executor £4. To the reparations of the Gaunts church, 40s. To thereparations of the pipes to convey water 20s. To John Borowes, sexton of the cathedral church, a jacket of russell worsted. Executor to buy 6 new matresses to be given at his discretion to certain almshouses where he shall think most need, 24s. To be distributed at his burial to poor people where need is, 20s; at his month's mind, 20s and at his year's mind, 20s. At his burial a trental of masses to be kept to the sum of 40s; "my mynde and will is to have a dirage and masse the daie of my buryall" with 20 priests, which costs shall amount to 16s, at the month's mind likewise 16s and at the year's mind likewise 16s.

To his sister Elizabeth Harte £50 in ready money to be delivered to the relief and comfort of the said Elizabeth at discretion of executor, "that it may be for hir relief and comforte in hir old age". To Charles Harte "my Sisters ——". merchant in Bristol £20 —— executor when the time of —— "Item my mynde and will is —— the oon half of my housh—— happen to departe owte of this —— apprentiswike my mynde ——".

Endorsed John Hollyday, William Babb

2 AGNES SAWNDERS, widow, St. Augustine, 22 May 1568, not proved.

Soul to almighty God, "trustinge to be saved only by the Deathe and passione of our savioure Jesus christ", body to Christian burial.

Goods equally divided between son John and daughter Elizabeth Sawnders, executors.

3   ELIZABETH DOLE, late wife of Thomas Dole, deceased, St. Peter, 8 April 1570, not proved.

Soul to almighty God and to the company and fellowship of all the blessed saints and angels in heaven. Body to be buried amongst "my other bretherne and Sisterne" in body of St. Peter's church near where late husband is buried. To cathedral church of St. "Awstens" [Augustine's] in Bristol 2s. To the poor men's box in the parish church of St. Peter's 3s 4d.

To Joan daughter of her son Ralph (Raphe) Dole one featherbed with appurtenances standing in her middle chamber. To Susan Roan daughter of her daughter Joan Roanes [*sic*] one other featherbed with appurtenances in the same chamber. To Elizabeth daughter of said Ralph one featherbed with appurtenances in the same chamber. To daughter Joan Roan standing bed which stands "in my newe Chamber alias the newe hall" and the truckle bed belonging to the same standing at the further end of the same chamber, with its appurtenances. The other bed and truckle bed with appurtenances in the hither end of the same chamber to son Ralph Dole.

To her daughter Joan Roan she gives her right and term of years in the house in which Joan dwells in Wine St. next to the house of Richard Goodyere, smith, on one side and the house of widow Haynes on the other side; the lease has already been given to Joan. To Maud wife of Richard Pittes one pair of woollen blankets. To William, youngest son of her son Ralph Dole, the greatest crock upon the shelf in the kitchen. To said Ralph the title of her 4 acres of meadow in the Marsh and to her daughter Joan Roan the title to 2 acres of meadow there. To "my buoye bryant" 6s 8d. To Christopher [D]everoux, curate of St. Peter's, 3s 4d for writing this will.

Residue equally to son Ralph Dole and daughter Joan Roan.

Debts owing by Elizabeth Dole:
to her baker Goodwife West, widow, £22 10s
to her brewer William Shuttle £6 10s
to Mr. Cole in the High Street 30s
to her son-in-law William Roan £10
to her son Ralph Dole £8

Witnesses: Richard Ashehurste, Roger Haynes, Robert Ufforde, whom she appoints overseers and to whom she makes a bequest for their pains.

[Note endorsed that the will not proved.]

4   FRANCIS COSTON, St. Nicholas, 9 November 1570, proved 10 May 1571.

Soul to almighty God, body to be buried "in the yearth".

To son Lewis £6 13s 4d. To daughter Alice Coston £6 13s 4d. Residue after debts paid to wife Anne, sole executrix.

Witnesses: Hugh Jones, weaver, William Abevan, tailor, of St. Nicholas.

5   EDWARD APOWELL, victualler, St. Nicholas, nuncupative, 22 August 1571, proved 19 October 1571.

Soul to the hands and mercy of God almighty, his only redeemer and saviour; body to Christian burial.

To daughter Mary (Marie) Apowell the best featherbed, the best flockbed and "a golde-ringe havinge a red stone with an Anticke". To father-in-law Anthony Goodyere, best gown of puke faced with budge.

Residue to wife Katherine Apowell, sole executrix.

Witnesses "hereunto presentt, and called" Morgan Harris, haulier, John Bonner, cardmaker, Anthony Goodyere, tailor, Welthian Betts and others.

6   CHRISTOPHER POWELL, Bristol, proved 1571.

Soul to almighty God, body to "the arthe".

To John More a pair of russet hose. To Walbroke of Bedminster a coat. To Richard Mollinor a dagger and a pair of knives.

Residue to wife, sole executrix.

[*Two copies of will, one without probate endorsement.*]

7   WILLIAM STONE, Temple, 8 April 1571, proved 22 June 1571.

Soul to almighty God and body to be buried in the parish churchyard of Temple.

All his goods to his wife whom he makes "whole" executrix to see his children honestly and virtuously brought up and to see [his body] honestly brought "in Earthe".

Witnesses: Richard Barwicke, vicar, John Lews and Roger Dere with others.

8   HARRY MAY, St. Nicholas, 9 June 1573, nuncupative, proved 25 August 1573.

"First he said, I knowe I shall nowe dye and not recover and there is but one way with me And therfore touchinge my worldly goodes, So it is that I broughte litle or nothinge to my wyffe Katheryn, And therfore I will not take or geve any thinge from her, but do refere all to her discretion amd make her my executrix these beinge Witnesses hearunto Edwarde [*blank*] Mariner William Rawlinges Thomas Brytaine William Tyrer and Jane Here".

Administration granted to wife Katherine executrix.

9 JOAN BECK, widow, St. Mary Redcliffe, 15 May 1574, proved 25 June 1574.

Soul to God the father and to his son Jesus Christ "by whose merites & bloud I stedfastly believe to be saved & to be inheritoure of the ioyes of heven withe the holy angeles"; body "to the earthe from whence it came believyying that I shall ryse agayne by the mightie powre of god at the day of iudgement incorruptible & immortall like unto the glorious body of Christ".

Goods to her servant William Henton, sole executor, to dispose the same as charity shall move him.

Witnesses: John Northbrooke, preacher, Thomas Owen, Richard Higgynes, Richard Dobbes and others.

10 JANE COMPANE alias FYANNE, widow, St. Stephen, 16 April 1574, proved 20 April 1574.

Soul "into the handes of my heavenly father in the merittes of the most paynfull passion precious deathe and Bloudsheddying of my lord and savyour Jesus Christe Amen". Body to Christian burial at the discretion of son Thomas Vyan.

To repairing of St. Stephen's church 3s 4d. To John Knyght "my gostly father" 20d. To the poor of St. Stephen 6s 8d.

To Katherine her servant 3s 8d. To Alice her servant "my Cassocke that I used to weare overmoste on the workyng dayes". To Margery Hopkins "my Cassocke that I used to weare under my sayd Cassocke".

Residue to son Thomas Vyan, executor.

Witnesses: John Knyght, clerk, Nicholas Woulffe and others.

Debt owed to Thomas ——— 4s.
Debt owed to testator by "goodwyfe Reade" 4s.

11 WILLIAM EDWARDS, farrier, [St. Michael], 24 August 1574, proved 1 October 1574 before the Bishop of Bath and Wells.

Soul unto the hands of almighty God and body to be buried in the church-yard of St. Michael. To "the pore people of our parishe" 12d. To "the par-sone of our churche" 12d.

To son William Edwards one silver spoon. To daughter Jane one silver spoon. To neighbour Thomas Kilbie a furred frieze (fris) cassock. To William Cradocke his best "cape" [*perhaps meaning* cap].

Residue to wife Alice Edwardes, sole executrix.

Overseers: John Butlere and Philip James; for their pains 12d apiece.

Witnesses: Sir Francis Howgreve, Thomas Kilbie, William Cradocke and others.

Debts owed to St. Michael's church 8s 8d.

[*There are two copies of this will but one only, headed* "Jesus", *endorsed with probate.*]

12   SIMON HERBERT, brewer, [St. Michael], 29 June 1574, proved 1 July 1574.

Soul to almighty God and body to be buried in St. Michael's church.
    To Cathedral 4d. To "the xiii pore people of the 3 kinges of Culleine a peine a pece".
    To daughters Joan, Susanna, Thomasine and Mary 20s each.
    Residue to wife Margaret, sole executrix.

Witnesses: sir Francis Howgreve, Philip James, William Cradocke and others.

13   ALAN HYLL, merchant, [St. Stephen], 9 December 1574, proved 16 February 1574/5.

"I . . . do make and ordayne, this my present testam[ent] contayninge theirin, ny last wyll". Soul to almighty God and to saviour Jesus Christ; body to be buried in churchyard of St. Stephen at discretion of executrix.
    Residue to wife Maud, sole executrix.

Witnesses: Mr. Thomas Chester, merchant, John Knyght, curate of the same parish and William Spratt, merchant

14   WILLIAM HOPKYN, St. Mary Redcliffe, 18 April 1574, proved 5 May 1574.

Soul [to God] the father and his son Jesus Christ, body to the earth.
    To daughter Agnes 20s and [cloth] for a cassock. To daughter Margaret a bequest [*will damaged*]. To Thomas Packer "my holy day hoyse and new canvasse doublett, a new sheyrtt, my freyse Jerkyne and my holy day cappe".
    Residue to wife Maud, sole executrix to dispose of goods "as charitie shall move her".

Witnesses: John Thew, clerk, Richard Hyggyns and John Jonson with others.

15 GEORGE HUNT, whittawer, [St. James], 27 November 1574, proved 22 December 1574.

Testament, containing his last will. Soul to almighty God "my macker and to Jesus Christe his sonne and my saviorre and to the holye ghoste my sanctyfyer iii persons but one god throughe whome onlye I am created, by whome onlye I am saved and in whome onlye iustyfyed"; body to be buried in the parish church of St. James.

To John Clarcke, son-in-law, 20s. To daughter Ellen "on neste of goblettes with a kever" weighing 4 score and 6 ounces [*5 lb. 6 oz.*] at the day of her marriage and a standing bed with a featherbed, a flock-bed with 2 pillows and his second best coverlet with a pair of sheets and a pair of blankets. To his daughter's daughter Constance a crock, a pan, a standing bed with a flock-bed, a featherbed, a pair of sheets and a covering.

To the poor of St. James's parish 20s to be divided among them in bread. His frieze gown to his servant John Wyllyams.

Residue to wife Agnes, sole executrix.

Overseers: John Bell and John Addams.

Witnesses: William Woolff "curate there", John Bell,vintner.

[Note with probate that Richard Clarke and John Clarke, pointmakers, bound.]

16 AGNES LEWIS/LEUES, widow, Christchurch, 13 January 1574/5, proved 28 January 1574/5.

Soul to almighty God, "my maker and redemer by whose deathe and passyon I trust to be savyd", body to be buried in Christchurch.

To her son Thomas Gwyne "all the Goodes that ys over and above one Inventry takyn by Wylliam Colstonne and Thomas Tycles that only to remayne accordinge to my late hosbandes wyll".

Son Thomas to be sole "executryxe".

Witnesses: Richard Hows [man], Robert Pestone, John Lewis, Thomas Holland, with others.

Endorsed: note re inventory, John Holland and John Lewis, glovers, being bound.

17 JOHN LEWIS, senior, pointmaker, Christchurch, 15 October 1571, proved 16 August 1574.

Soul to almighty God "my maker and redemer by the merittes of whose Passion I faithfullye truste to inherit the kingedome of Heaven"; body to be buried in the churchyard of St. James within the suburbs of the city.

All goods and chattels to wife Agnes Lewes to enjoy and use during her natural life; any remaining after her death (his debts being paid) to son John Lewes, executor.

Overseers: "my master John Jacobbe Poyntmaker" and Henry Marwell, glover.

Witnesses: Hugh Harvye, Nicholas Badyere.

18   RICHARD NEWMAN, butcher, St. Nicholas, 7 December 1574, proved 4 March 1574/5.

"I . . . do ordayne and make this my pressent test[ament] Contaynyng theryn my laste wyll"

Soul to almighty God his creator, redeemer and saviour, and to all the holy glory of the celestial company of heaven, by whose death and passion he is saved. Body to be buried in St. Nicholas churchyard at the discretion of the overseers.

To poor 20s in money or bread.

To wife Ursula the lease of his dwelling house with household stuff and implements; wife discharged from paying or receiving any of his debts. To daughter Alice £26 13s 4d to be paid at her marriage, "yff she lyve thereto", Edmund his son to pay her out of the profits of "my leaces that I gev hym". If Alice die before marriage then her legacy to son Edmund.

To son Edmund all his leases of tenements, stables, land or boards (bordes), and all debts owing to testator. Edmund to give Alice £26 13s 4d out of the profits of the leases. If Edmund die before age of 21 or before Alice marries then all the leases to remain to Alice. If Edmund and Alice die before coming of age then all leases to remain to wife Ursula.

Residue to son Edmund and wife Ursula, executrix.

Overseer: William Hopkyn, fishmonger.

19   ROLAND NORTHALL, St. Mary Redcliffe, 30 April 1574, proved 1 October 1574.

Soul to almighty God, saviour and redeemer and body to be buried in Redcliffe churchyard. To "the poore mans boxe" 4d. Goods and chattels not yet given and bequeathed, to wife Elizabeth, executrix; "she to pay my dettes & receave my dettes & to see me honestly buried".

Witnesses: Mr. John Northbroke, preacher, Davy Williams, curate of Redcliffe with others.

20 WILLIAM TURNER, weaver, St. Thomas, 10 May 1574, proved 21 May 1574.

Soul to God the father and his son Jesus Christ, "by whose merites and vertue of his passion [and resur]rection [*will damaged*] I have and shall have remission and forgyvnes of my synnes —— everlastinge and to ryse agayne at the day of iudgement by the mightie powre of god". Body to the earth.

To son Thomas four looms with all things belonging to them, a standing bed, a flock bed with bolster and all things belonging. "Thies parcels above rehersed" to be kept by wife Maud until Thomas attains the age of 24, then the looms to be made "as good in all poyntes as they were at the day of my buryall and so to be delyvered".

To daughter Alice (Alls) a cupboard, a great crock and 20s to be kept by his wife Maud until Alice's marriage.

Residue to wife Maud, sole executrix, "to gyve and dispose the same as charitie shall move her".

Witnesses: John Thew, curate, William Appric[e] and Richard Smythe with others.

Bondsmen: William Howell of Redcliffe, linen weaver and William Apprice of St. Thomas, glover.

21 EDWARD WAWEN, St. Mary Redcliffe, 8 May 1574, proved 12 May 1574.

Soul to God the father; by the merits of Jesus Christ, his passion and resurrection hopes to have forgiveness of sins, life everlasting and his body to rise [again] at the day of judgement and general resurrection and in the meantime to go to the earth from whence it came.

Goods to be divided into 2 by 2 honest men. His wife Joan to take which part "shall like her best"; the other part, being for daughter Susan, is to remain in Joan's hands until Susan's marriage.

Said wife Joan to be sole executrix; supervisor, Thomas Owen, sen.

Witnesses: Thomas Owen, William Huntt and others.

22 WILLIAM YEMAN, glover, Bristol, 21 December [?1573], proved 5 April 1574.

Soul to almighty God his redeemer and saviour. Body to Christian burial.

To son William 3 houses, 2 in St. Peter's parish, one in Broadmead, St. James, with all implements and appurtenances, and £20 with his best goblet.

Custody of son William bequeathed to William Yeman, jun. grocer.

To daughters Alice, Margaret, Katherine and Joan £20 each. To Katherine "my base daughter" £5. Sums to be paid at the age of 20 years;

if any daughter die before this then her legacy to be divided among the others.
    Unspecified legacy to father John Yeman [*will damaged*].
    Residue to ?wife Joan, executrix, [*will damaged*].

Overseer: William Yeman, jun. grocer.

23   MORGAN DAVIS, wireworker, St. Mary Redcliffe 19 February 1591/2, proved in P.C.C. 24 March 1592/3.

Soul to almighty God and body to the earth whence it came, to be buried in Redcliffe churchyard.
    All goods to wife Alice, sole executrix, desiring her to see his body honestly brought to earth.

Witnesses: Thomas Rider, curate of Redcliffe, Alice Rider and others.

Administration granted to Alice Davys, widow of deceased.

24   AGNES ANDROWS, widow, Bristol, 6 July 1593.

Deed of gift, filed with other wills by Registry. Agnes Androws was executrix of will of Humphrey Androws, deceased, which has not survived in this series of wills.
    One silver penny to each of her children.
    attached: schedules of money, goods and plate given to each child, this being additional to legacies received by the will of their father Humphrey Androws.
    To son Humphrey Androws: £60 to be paid when his other legacies from father's will are due. If he die before then the gift to be void. Her best goblet of silver gilt weighing 19oz to be delivered with father's legacies. If he die before then the gift to be divided equally between his brother and sisters. Agnes Andrews to have use of the goblet for life.
    To son John Andrews: £60 under conditions as above. Her second best goblet of silver gilt weighing 19oz under conditions as above. All the "wainskott draperie and cobberttes fastened in weinskott glasse glasse windowes the table bordes with their frames and the stooles and side bordes in the too parlors being nowe in the dwelling house which was late new bilte in Wine Street there to remayne as standers and ynplementes to the howse"
    To daughter Abigail Andrews: £60 under conditions as above. Her third best goblet of silver gilt weighing 19oz as above.
    To daughter Anne Andrews: £60 under conditions as above. Her best salt with silver gilt cover weighing 23oz as above. Lease and term of years on tenement in Wine Street occupied by John Goslett, goldsmith, and garden near Mumbridge in Bristol, "which shalbe unexpired at the deth of the said Anne the mother".

Endorsed: "Sealed and delyvered this present dede, severally to the children within named, together also with the possession of the parcells of plate, and a penny of silver in the name of possession of the same, and all thinges within specified".

Witnesses: Humphrey Clovill, John Butcher.

25 DAVID BARNES, tucker, Temple 12 July 1593, proved 13 August 1593.

Sick in body, bequeaths soul to God almighty and body to the earth "And verilye hope throughe the deathe and passion of my savioure Jesus Christe & his bloode sheed for me to have remission of my sinnes and to enioye his kingdome prepared for me & for all those that beleve in him".

All goods, after payment of debts, to wife Joan, sole executrix; nephews William Barnes and John Barnes, overseers.

Witnesses: Richard Marten, vicar of Temple, Mr. John Barnes, alderman, Thomas Beese, Anthony Hedges with others.

26 ALICE BATTEN, St. Werburgh, 3 May 1591, nuncupative, admon. granted 30 August 1591 [*endorsement 1593*].

All goods and legacies to cousin Mary Batten, daughter of John Batten of St. Werburgh, carpenter.

Witnesses: Lewis Davys of St. Werburgh and Alice his wife, Avis Morgann, Elizabeth Rothe and Katherine Smythe.

27 HARRY BEYMAND, dyer, St. James, 15 April 1590, proved 20 July 1593.

Soul to God almighty and body to the earth.

All goods to wife Joan, sole executrix, who is to pay charges of his burial; "to this brieffe will & Testament I the said Harrye Beymand have sett my firme".

Witnesses: Nicholas Gloide, William Thomas, Abraham Hawkes

28 DARBYE CAROWE, petty chapman, St. Mary Redcliffe, 10 July 1593, proved 7 September, 1593.

"the xxvth year of the Raygne of our soveraygne Ladye Ellysabeth of Inglond France and yearlond queene defenderest of The most awntyent catholyke fayth".

Soul to almighty God. Body to be buried in Redcliffe churchyard.

To Philip Blake, son of Alexander Blake, his best bed with all its furniture, and best bedstead. Also "a yower and a Bason and a good Crocke", to be delivered to him after decease of testator's wife, "yf she doe not of necessytie spend yt upon hyr selffe".

To John Moollyns his son-in-law, 12s and his debts. To Magdalene Welshe, daughter of James Welshe, 20s to be paid at testator's wife's decease.

Residue to wife Ellen, sole executrix.

Overseers: William Benne, Alexander Blake.

29   RICHARD CLERKE, pointmaker, St. James, nuncupative, July 1591, proved 28 September 1593.

Memorandum that "uppon one day happeninge in the moneth of Julye laste paste 1591 Richard Clerke . . . beinge moved by Thomas Twynborow Clerke to make his Testament or laste will" devised that son John should have all his goods, chattels, debts and lands and he would refer the disposition of them only to the good discretion and government of his said son whom he appointed sole executor.

Witnesses: Mr. Twynborow with others.

30   THOMAS COLLINS, freemason, London and Bristol, St. Philip, 21 January 1593/4, proved 15 February 1593/4.

Soul to almighty God, body to be buried in chancel of St. Philip's church.

To cousin Alice Cole of Itchingferry, Southampton, a feather bed, a bolster, a pillow, a woven covering and a pair of sheets, one brass pot, a "chaffen", a skimmer, a rug mantle, three of his best chests and one white rug coverlet.

To Alice's husband Thomas Cole a black jerkin of sealskin and a pair of blue breeches. To Peter Chadwicke a jerkin of spotted sealskin, and to Peter's son "all my free stone at Denmeade lyinge in a backsyde of one Henrie Foster", and a little pocket dagger.

To William Hanbye all his free stone at Temple Gate and Redcliffe Hill, both Bath and Dundry stone, and all his stone at the Three Cornish Choughs at the Key, also all his chimneys at John Dakers in Corn Street, and at "goodman Jeffris with the Dioll". Also his best jerkin, doublet and breeches, and three chests with three boxes.

To Joan Hanbye, wife of William Hanbie, his greatest flockbed and bolster, his best cloak and one chest. To Margaret Hanbie, daughter of William Hanbye, his lesser flockbed and bolster, one old rug coverlet, a plot of garden in Old Market adjoining the house of John Tomson, tanner, and house of John Bolwell, rough layer, and a joined chair and a chest.

To John Dakers all his old lead and solder in the house. To Anthony Vaughan two "dagges" [?daggers]. To Robert Chocke, freemason, a pair of round leather breeches. To William Hanbie, freemason, one of his best axes and one and a half dozen tools. To John Frinde, Richard Gardner, Anthony Frende, Richard Chocke and Simon Batten, freemasons, one axe and a dozen tools each.

To John Lay, haulier, his testament book. To John Frende his pen and inkhorn with all his drawing tools. "Item I give my bookes of byldinge unto John Frynde and Anthony Frynde, freemasons, with my draught plottes to be devided accordinge to the discrecion of John Frynde or my owne selfe".

To John Warde of Siston (Sison) a pair of black leather boots and a pair of spurs.

Residue to William Hanbye, freemason, "whole" executor, to receive and pay all debts.

Overseers: Anthony Vaughan, smith, William Hanby, freemason, John Warde, rough layer.

31   OWEN COLWAYE, surgeon, St. Stephen, 17 November 1593, *no probate but endorsed* 1593.

Weak in body, bequeaths soul "into the keping of the Almyghty god my Creator Jesus Christ my Redemer, And the holly sperit proseding of them both my Sanctyfyer & gwyderes". Body to be buried in parish church of St. Stephen.

To son John Colwaye the debts and pawns which Sir Finen O Driscoll owes testator. Residue to wife Maud, sole executrix.

Witness: Arthur Panthur

32   THOMAS DALLOWE, tailor, St. John, 27 September 1593, nuncupative, admon. granted 5 October, 1593.

All his goods, chattels and debts equally divided between four children of his cousin Richard Blundye, hooper: John, Richard, Mary and Margery.

Witnesses: John Eddye, cooper, Margaret Williams "who kept hym in his sicknes", James Owen his servant and others.

Admon. with will annexed granted to Richard Blundey during minority of four children, as no executor named in will.

33   LEWIS DAVIS, St. Philip in the suburbs of the City of Bristol, 25 August 1593, proved 7 September 1593.

Commends his soul to almighty God whom he acknowledges to be his maker and redeemer and his body to be buried in St. Philip's churchyard. To the poor of the same parish 2s to be distributed amongst them in bread.

Residue to wife Margaret, sole executrix, provided that testator's son-in-law John Harte shall have the same after her decease for the better execution of this will.

Overseers: trusty friends John Harvey of the parish of Publey [Publow] and Nicholas Chambers who are to have 6d apiece for a token.

Witnesses: Thomas Harvye, Richard Wrighte.

Debts owing to testator:
John Powell of Stanton, Wilts. £2 4s
Richard Wright of Bristol, draper £6 "Whereof I receaved ijs".

34   THOMAS DAVIS, hooper, St. Stephen, 25 December 1593, proved 15 February 1593/4.

Soul to almighty God "of whom I do not doubt, But that hee of his meere mercie and greate goodnes will forgive mee my sins, And make mee A perpetuall Inheritour with him of the Everlastinge Joyes of heavin". Body to be buried in St. Stephen's churchyard near his son's grave.

Wife Agnes to pay his son Harry £10 if she marry again. Wife to give son Harry "the great cheaste at the stayer headd", and a joined bedstead with a flock bed and all things necessarie". Wife to have use of them until she marry. After that testator's brother John Davis to have custody of son Harry and goods until he comes of age.

To husband of his sister Joan a black cloth doublet. To brother John Davis his best breeches. To the two daughters of his brother John 10s each.

Residue to wife Agnes, executrix.

Witnesses: John Davis, hooper, Thomas Tyzon, parson of St. Stephen's.

35   FRANCIS DENNYS, gent. of the Hundred of Barton by Bristol in the county of Gloucestershire, 13 January 35 Eliz. [1592/3], proved 16 June 1593.

"I bequeath unto Almightie god my sowle the maker & redeemer thereof" and body to be buried in the church of St. Philip within the suburbs of the city.

To godson Francis Stone son of Edmond Stone an annuity of 5 marks p.a. out of the manor of Bodington, Gloucs. during the life of John Read jun. of the same county which testator bought of John Read, but if John

Read pay Francis Stone £5 he shall have his annuity again. Also to Francis Stone his godson one heifer which has not yet calved and all the corn already sowed or "which shalbe sowed at the hower of my dethe". Also to him the mead ground hired and paid for of my neighbour Jelicote; if Jelicote pay Francis Stone the 30s which testator paid him for the same a month before mowing time then he is to enter into his mead ground again.

As his godson is very young and out of discretion, those who will take upon them to take into their hands the same portion testator has given him, shall put in reasonable assurance to his overseers to answer for the same when the boy is 16 years and then to bind the boy apprentice; testator hopes they will keep the boy at school "at least wyse to write reade & cast Accompt".

Residue to Mary Dennys daughter of Katherine Lluellin now dwelling with Mistress Mary Dennys in St. Augustine's Green, sole executrix, provided that in her marriage she follows advice of William Lluellyn of Westerleigh and Robert Murseley of Dyrham.

Overseers cousin John Dennys of Pucklechurch and John Roe "desiringe them to advise the mayde the best they cann"; 3s 4d apiece for their pains.

Memorandum: 16 Jan. year aforesaid, testator read this will to cousin Francis Dennys "who liked so well thereof that he desired me to putt my hand thereunto for a wytnes". Will read before John Denys, William Shipward, James Rogers

Addition to will, 20 Jan.
To the poor of St. Philip's 13s 4d. To his servant Margaret 13s 4d for the pains she has taken with him during his sickness. Overseers to see him buried "as my neihbors ar buryed & no otherwyse" the charge thereof to be borne with money in his coffer at the hour of his death.

Witness: John Denys

Debts owing to testator:
lent to cousin Chester "out of my purse" 33s
lent to him at his going to the court £4
Anthony Vaughan, smith, for coal he had of testator 38s
the smith over against Vaughan for coal 4s 6d
lent out of his purse to Edward Stone 20s
Hawkins the truss carrier for hay and lent out of testator's purse 24s 4d
to neighbour William Cory and lent out of testator's purse 6s
to William Coates, deceased, lent out of testator's purse for a truss of hay 7s
to Benbowe the baker, money due in part of payment of a horse testator sold him 6s
George Skull owes 20s
the brewer of the steps in Horsestreet for coal which testator's servant delivered 12s 8d
Tucker, lent out of testator's purse 4s
Morris Kidd, lent out of testator's purse 5s

left with Anthony Morman in his keeping £6 13s 4d
Robert Cory 40s
John Byn for a truss of hay 7s 6d
William Jervies for a truss of hay 8s
John Avery for a truss of hay 8s
Robert Gunyng lent out of testator's purse 4s
William Curties owes for boards 52s

36   CHRISTIAN ELLIOT, widow, St. Philip, 3 September 1593, admon. granted 11 September 1593.

Soul to almighty God, her Maker, Saviour and Redeemer. Body to be buried in St. Philip's churchyard near to the graves of John Elonde and his wife.

To poor of parish 20s to be distributed at the discretion of the overseers.

To Nicholas Chambers, William Abraham and Joan Taylor in St. Mary le Port Street, widow, a bushel of rye each. To daughter Dorothy her best feather bed, best feather bolster, best covering, and the coffer that stands "at my bedes feete with all that is in him" and a bedstead.

To son William the bed "which I nowe lye on", her second bolster, second coverlet and bedstead "wherein I lye". To brother Thomas Elonde a bushel of rye. To Edith Bucke a platter: To Christian Bucke, daughter of Richard Bucke, a platter, a candlestick and saucer. To Gillian Bucke her best crock.

Residue to son William [Jones *deleted*] Elliot and daughter Dorothy, "full and whole" executors.

All former wills revoked.

Overseers: Richard Bucke, Harry Smythe, each to receive 3s 4d.

Admon. granted to Richard Bucke and Edward Elliott during minority of executors, as also were letters of guardianship of the minors. Inventory valued at £12 1s 8d.

37   HELEN FORD, widow, St. Nicholas, 13 (Ides) December 1590, proved 31 August 1593.

Soul into the hands of almighty God; body to be buried in St. Stephen's churchyard.

Worldly goods as follows: to Mary White her daughter's daughter one featherbed, 2 feather bolsters, one feather pillow, one little spruce chest, one tablecloth of dowlas of a breadth and a half, one dozen napkins of the same cloth wrought with blue, 5 pairs of sheets, one pair of pillow-beres and a buttery door cloth, one brazen pan the third [?best], one gridiron, one red rug coverlet, one dripping pan, one frying pan, one little carpet, one broach, 6 platters, one charger, 2 pewter "porrenge" dishes, 3 saucers, one pottinger, one brass crock, 2 curtains of flannen, one tester of red say (sayes) and green.

All the above goods are left in the custody of Robert Deane, hooper, to the use of said Mary until the age of 18 or marriage. If it please God to call said Mary by death to his mercy before the age of 18 years or before her marriage, the above goods are to remain to testatrix's daughter's son George Crump or if the said George also die, then to remain to Robert Deane who is to pay testatrix's sister Elizabeth Adams 10s.

To sister Elizabeth Adams all her apparel, one pair of coarse sheets, one red coverlet for a bed. To her daughter Joan one platter and one bell candlestick. To George Crump her garden lying in St. James's parish.

Residue to said George, sole executor, to receive and pay debts.

Debts owing "unto other":
to John Fyld and Robert Deane £3
to the goodman Rockwell, brewer 3s 6d
to "my mayde Lyllie White" 17s

Debts due to her:
John Williams of Newport for victuals 9s 4d
John Man of St. Maryport for victuals 4s 11d
the same John for 2 years' bedding 26s
Thomas Davies alias Penny, merchant, for 25 weeks lodging 8s 4d

Overseers of this last will and testament, John Field and Robert Deane

Witnesses: myself Helen Ford, George Harris, vicar, Elizabeth Lyllywhite, "Edye" Bowen.

[*This will was annexed to the commission to Mary White to administer.*]

38 ANNE FREELYNGE, widow, St. Peter, 8 October 1593, proved 10 November 1593. Soul to almighty God. Body to be buried in church by [*beside*] her husband.

To Walter Lypett all her goods, executor, "he to see me honestlye brought in earthe".

Witnesses: Frances Garlande, Agnes Williams and others.

39 ANTHONY GOODYERE, tailor, Bristol, 31 August. 1592, proved 2 March 1593/4.

(Deed of Gift)
"Be it knowne unto all men by theese presentes that I Anthonye Goodyere of the cittie of Bristoll Taylor, beine now sick in bodye and mindinge the benefitt and good preferment of my welbeloved wife Joan Goodyer, to be for her quitnes after my decease, Do therefor by theese name and elect my verye trustie Frend Rice Tanner yoman in this behalfe, and also I do by theese presentes geve graunt and Deliver unto him the said Rice Tanner only of trust for the use and benefitt of my said wife

Joan Goodyere" all parcels of goods, implements and household stuff expressed in the schedule or paper annexed to these presents to hold to the said Rice Tanner, to the benefit and use of said wife Joan Goodyer for evermore "Frely to disspose it as her owen proper goods without any cleaime or challenge or demaunde to be had made or done to the same or any parte thereof byme the said Anthony Goodyere my executors or administrators at any time hearafter And I do deliver to the said Rice Tanner one Kettle parcell of the premisses in the name of full possession of all the rest of the said goods specified in the said schedull".

Witnesses: John Wyllmott, Lewis Awbrye and Morgan Jones, the writer hereof, and Anthony Vaughan with others.

[*The schedule is not annexed.*]

40   JOHN JAMES, tailor, St. Stephen, 22 November 1593, proved 14 December, 1593.

Soul to almighty God, "of whome I doe not doubt but that hee will of his mere mercie, forgive mee my Sinnes, And make my soule A perpetuall Inheritour withe him of the Everlastinge Joyes of heavin". Body to be buried in St. Stephen's churchyard.

To daughter Alice Busher, widow, a flock bed, a pair of sheets, a blanket and a coverlet. Also "my greate ponne".

Residue to wife Dorothy, "full and hole executrix".

Witnesses: John Fine, Richard Snacknayle, Thomas Tyzon, parson of St. Stephen's, and others.

41   THOMAS JONES, St. Thomas 24 October 1593, proved 14 December 1593.

Sick in body, bequeaths soul into the hands of God that made it "not doubtinge of remission of sinnes through the death & passion of christ my redeemer"; body to be buried in the churchyard of St. Thomas in christian burial.

To son Walter Jones one flock-bed and bolster, one pair of sheets, one coverlet, all testator's apparel and his working tools.

Residue to wife Margaret Jones, sole executrix. Desires William Edwin and James Newton to take upon them to be overseers.

The mark of Thomas Jones.

Witnesses: Samuel Davis, vicar, William Hyll.

42   JONAS LACYE, clerk, Bristol, 18 October 1591, nuncupative, admon. annexed 13 November 1591, [*endorsement 1593*].

All his goods and chattels to mother Margery Wall alias Lacy, "in consideracion that he had his only mainteynance and attendaunces in his sicknes, at his said mothers hands".

Witness: Morgan Jones, parson of Christchurch, with others.

43   GEORGE LAURENCE, of the parish of St. Stephen's and clerk of the parish of All Saints 18 October 1593, proved 24 November 1593.

Soul to the hands of almighty God "of whome I doe not doubt, but that he of his meere mercye, will forgeve me my sinnes, & make me a perpetuall inheritour with him of the everlastinge ioyes in heaven". Body to be buried in the parish church of All Saints.
    All his goods to his wife, whom he makes "executrix full".
    "And this I end upon Thursday beinge the eightenth day of October, & the xxxv th yeare of the raigne of owr Sovereine and vertuous Queene Elizabeth".

Witnesses: Elizabeth Wine, Anne Davis, widow

44   GILLIAN A PENDRYE, widow, St. Thomas, 7 September 1593, proved 17 January 1593/4.

Soul to almighty God "my Creatour and Redemer to Remayne with him in perfect felicity". Body to the earth.
    To St. Thomas Church 6d. To the poor of the hospital or almshouse in "Longe Rewe" 6d.
    To daughter Ann Appendry a chest bound with iron standing in the hall, left by her grandmother. Also a brass pan and brass pot left by her grandmother.
    Lease of her house and residue of goods to daughter Joan A Pendrye, executrix.

Overseers: Samuel Davis, vicar, William Lavington, gent.

Witnesses: Thomas Byssop, William Morgan.

45   KATHERINE FESAUNT, *endorsed* PHEASANT, widow, [St. Stephen] 1593, proved 16 January 1593/4.

Soul into the hands of almighty God and body to be buried in St. Stephen's parish.
    To son John Fessaunt the second feather bed, one pair of sheets, the best coverlet, a bolster and a gold ring with the Roman letters and 40s in money to be paid by Thomas Mason, baker.

To servant Alice Ditheridg one flock-bed, one bolster of feathers, one pair of sheets, 3 rugs for a bed, one kettle, a petticoat with the "Mocado bodies", one partlet, one dozen of trenchers and 20s in money to be paid by Thomas Mason aforesaid.

To daughter Anne Fessaunt all that remains, viz. 2 featherbeds and a flock-bed, 7 white and grey rugs, 2 pair of blankets, 3 red mantles, 6 pair of sheets, 3 pillows, 3 pillow-beres and 11 partlets, 5 double kerchiefs (carthars) and 11 corner kerchiefs, 7 table napkins, one bread napkin, 4 towels, one tablecloth, 7 smocks, 4 gowns, 3 petticoats, 2 hats, 6 yards of medley cloth, one pair of curtains, one standing bedstead, 3 bedsteads, a little spruce chest, 3 other chests, one little box, 3 chairs, one straw chair, one spruce board with the frame, one long table board, 6 stools, one cupboard (colbert), 8 platters, 5 pottingers, 8 saucers, 2 present pots, one pewter bottle, 6 "floure pottes", 4 candlesticks, one spice mortar, a quart and a pint pot, one bowl basin, a great brass pan, 2 crocks, 3 skillets, one kettle, one chafing-dish, one skimmer, one frying pan, 3 broaches, one gridiron, a pair of andirons (Anndyars), a pair of dogs, one pair of pothooks, one pair of tongs, 13 handkerchiefs, one ell of holland in 2 pieces, half an ell of "Kalikeene", half an ell of cambric, 3 dozen of trenchers "the lese of the house", 3 gold rings, £8 money, 4 aprons and 2 silk girdles and she is to be full and whole executrix of this will.

Witnesses: Thomas Mason, Thomas Taylor with others.

46   ROBERT RISBY, Barton Hundred, 3 December 1592, proved 2 June 1593.

Soul to almighty God. Body to be buried in St. Peter's Church.

To wife Dorothy the house in St. Maryport Street or annual rent of 40s for life, a joined bedstead in the back chamber, and all his pewter and brass in the house. To his wife all his household stuff in his house at Deanridg in Barton Hundred, also the government of his son Christopher until he is 16, and 1 dozen silver spoons.

To son Christopher the fee simple of his house in St. Maryport Street, then to his heirs; in default of heirs to Thomas Risby, son of Nicholas Risby, testator's son; in default of his heirs to next of kin.

To son Christopher the glass windows, wainscot and "drapery ware'" in his house in Bristol, and two joined table boards "thoon in the parlor thother in the halle", four joined forms belonging to the tables, a cupboard in the parlour, two joined bedsteads "thon in the halle thother in the back chamer", the iron bars and the feather bed, and his silver double gilt goblet.

To daughter Joan Wigons 50s.

To the poor 10 dozen "of bred" to be given at his burial.

Residue to wife Dorothy and son Christopher, executors.

Overseers: John Burnell, Thomas Jenyngs.

Witnesses: Thomas Fido, John Burnell, Thomas Jennynges and others.

47 NICHOLAS ROBYNS, tailor, St. Mary le Port, nuncupative 6 February 1592/3, proved 27 March 1592 [*recte* 1593; *endorsed* 1593].

Sick in body, commends soul into the hands of almighty God his creator, hoping only to be saved by his great mercy through the merits, death and passion of Jesus Christ "my redeemer & alone savyour". Body to be buried in the churchyard of St. Mary le Port.

All goods to his wife Amyee Robins, his debts paid and funeral discharged, whom he makes sole executrix.

Witnesses: Richard Arthur, clerk, Edward Evenet, Henry Whytaker, John Phyllips, John Veysee etc.

Debts owed by testator: to the parish for rent and monies borrowed £2 10s

48 THOMAS ROGERS, tanner, St. Mary Redcliffe, 28 May 1593, proved July [?24, *date partially blotted*] 1593.

Soul to almighty God, body to be buried in Redcliffe churchyard.

To cathedral church of St. Austens [St. Augustine's] 4d.

Residue to wife Elizabeth "whome I do make my hole ececcytryx shee to see my bodye honestly browght unto the Earth".

Overseers: William Benne, Samson Borges, to have 6d each.

49 ELIZABETH SCULLICK, widow, St. Augustine the Less 8 October 1589, proved 5 February 1590/1, [*endorsed 1593*].

Soul to almighty God and body to be buried in the parish church of "Littill St. Austins".

To her daughter Maud, lease of testatrix's dwelling house, the bed "that I doe lie on" and a table board. To John Coocke, eldest son of daughter Joan, a tablecloth. To children of Richard Coocke all her linen, brass and pewter.

Overseers: Richard Coocke and Thomas Batten.

Witnesses: Richard Coocke, Thomas Batten, Joan Coocke "and I Thomas Johnes vicare of the parishe".

Proved by Richard Cooke and Maud Scolick.

50 RICHARD SHORE, yeoman, St. James, 26 November 1593, proved 26 January 1593/4.

Body to the earth, "trusting to be saved onlie by the presious death and blode seadinge my onlie Savioure and redemer by whose death onlie I hope to be saved and by noe other meanes".

To daughter Mary a silver cup called a beaker, parcel gilt. To daughters Cicely and Mary £25 each, to be paid at 21 years or marriage, whichever is first. If either die before this, "then she so liveinge to have her parte dienge".

To wife Alice the messuage he now lives in for a term of ten years, paying the lord's rent, residue to son William. If he die before ten years, residue to be divided equally between the two daughters.

To Anne Shore, daughter of his brother William Shore, a yearling "in a token of my good will". To her mother "an angell of golde".

To son William his second bedstead and feather bed "to be delivered at the discrecion of my executrix", a spruce chest and a spruce counter, and the lease of the pavement in Turn Againe Lane "which I bought of Mr. Pryn", also his wain bound with iron, a "sollowe with his Iren" and a dray.

Residue to wife Alice, sole executrix.

Overseer: William Shore, to have 20s.

"And thus I make an end forsakeinge all other wills by me herto fore made".

Witnesses: Willliam Shore; Elizabeth Sweper, Thomas Langley.

51   JOHN TAWNYE, bowyer, Christchurch 15 September 1593, proved 28 November 1593.

"Consideringe that all persons are borne to dye, & that the time of the same is not knowen unto any savinge unto the almightie god, do therefore aswell for the declaracion of my faith in god, as also for the orderlye distributinge & disposinge of that poore talent of worldlye goodes wherewith he of his mere goodnes hath endued me declare this my testament".

Soul "to the almightie god my maker & creator, assuredlye belevinge, that by the onlye merites of the passion of his dear & welbeloved sonne my saviour & redemer, I shall inherite the celestiall Kingdome of heaven a place prepared for all suche as put theire trust in him". Body to be buried in the churchyard of Christchurch.

To Anne Grene daughter of son-in-law Richard Grene, testator's flock-bed that is in the "Coke lofte". To Mary and Bridget, daughters of John Warren, a platter each. To son-in-law William Hemynge "all my toles in my shope".

Residue to wife Agnes Tawnye and Jane Gwylliams whom he makes "executors"; goods to be equally divided between them. If the said Jane outlive her mother the said Agnes, she is to have the portion of his goods that will come to said mother's hands after her decease.

Witness: Morgan Jones, the writer hereof

Testator's mark: a bow and arrow.

Probate states that administration was granted to Anne Tawney, the testator's widow named in the will, who brought in an inventory to the value of £5 6 10d

The mark of John Tawnye, bowyer, used to authenticate his will

52   RICHARD WILLIAMS, St. Philip, 14 January 1592/3, nuncupative, proved 1593.

"Being requested by his wyffe to geve some what to his children, saied, That those goodes he had I geve and Bequeathe to Joane my wyffe (and all litle enoughe for her) whome I make myne Executrixe".

Witnesses: John Kyng and Elizabeth Kyng of St. James.

53   AGNES BAYLIE alias PITTS, Bristol 12 May 1596, proved 4 February 1597/8.

Now wife of Francis Baylye, late wife of William Pittes, deceased; sick in body.

Commits soul into the hands of God "my moste deare and lovinge father, beinge Constanttly assured throughe faythe, of my Salvatione in and throughe the merceyes and merretts of Jesus Christ his only begotten Sonne and my most merceyfoll savyoure and redemer, And my bodey to the Earthe, from whence ytt was takine, nothinge doughtinge of the Resurectione bothe of the soulle, and bodey att the laste Day unto Everlastinge lyf".

Goods due to her as executrix of last will of William Pyttes her late husband, to her present loving and dear husband Francis Baylie as follows: after her funeral discharged, residue "for the better bringinge upp of my Children". Said husband, sole executor.

Witnesses: George Myllner, Philip Cowper, Hugh (Hewe) Sysell

54 NICHOLAS BAYLYE, trumpeter, St. Stephen, 5 February 1596/7, proved 13 May 1597.

Soul to almighty God, body to be buried in St. Stephen's church.
  To poor of St. Stephen's 6s 8d.
  Residue to brother Thomas, sole executor, except for "my best Ringe which I have upon my fynger" to Joan Fowens, widow, and "my other rynge that is upon my fynger" to Joan Coulman.

Witnesses: Morgan Jones, clerk, John Fownes, Thomas Wyckham, Benedict Macham.

55 WILLIAM BOYDELL, merchant, [Christchurch] 29 November 1597, proved 16 December 1597.

"for as muche as death is to all men certayne & the houre thereof uncertayne" he makes his last will and testament. Sick in body; soul to God his maker, redeemer and saviour and his body to be buried as near as maybe to his mother's grave in Christchurch parish.
  To every one of his sister's children 20 – each to be delivered as each reaches 21 years. 6s 8d to a preacher to preach at his burial.
  Residue to brother-in-law Christopher Woodwarde, sole executor. Revokes former wills.

Witnesses: Henry Robertes, Morgan Jones. "By me Johane Didmuster".

56 HUGH CICILL, [carp]enter, St. Philip, 14 April 1597, proved 28 April 1597.

Soul to almighty God, body to be buried in St. Philip's church, beside his wife.
  [To son John Cicill] his best cloak, his breeches, best doublet, [2] pairs of shoes, a pair of buskins, 2 pairs of stockings, his best hat, a shirt, 2 "swoodes", a chest, a flockbed, a bolster, a coverlet, [a chair], a forest bill, a cleave, "my least kettle saving one", all his working tools, a pottinger, a saucer, a flowerpot, a pewter dish, a candlestick, [2] spoons and the lease of his house.
  To son-in-law [Ham]sheare his bow and arrows and "all that to them belongethe". To [daughter] Joan his second bedstead, 2 chests, a cupboard in the chamber, a pottinger, a fruit dish, a plate trencher, 2 candlesticks, a pewter dish, a chafing dish, a pint pot, a pewter drinking cup, a skimmer, a cruse, a pewter candlestick, a feather bed, a bolster, a bedcase, a pair of [sheets, a pair of] fine sheets, a pan, 2 kettles, a crock, a pillow, a pillowbere, a [tablecloth], a stained cloth, a coverlet, a red cradle cloth.
  To [daughter] Elizabeth Powell a worsted petticoat, a black cassock, a crock, "my wyves [best Showes] and hosen", an apron, a pottinger, a saucer.

To [daughter] Agnes Hamsheare a great kettle, "my wyves best Cassacke", a pair of sleeves, a [candlestick], a pottinger, a saucer, a flowerpot, 2 spoons, a cupboard in [the hall, a] chair, a bedstead, a bed, a bolster, 2 pairs of sheets, a pillow and [a coverlet].

To daughter Alice Cicill a bed, a bolster, a pair of sheets, a candlestick, a big salt cellar with a cover, a pewter dish, a flowerpot, 2 [spoons], a white waist petticoat, "my wyves best and second petticotes", a joined chest "at the [stairs head]", a fine sheet. To Alice also his best [bedstead], which his son John is to keep until she is married "or ells at that time to buye for her one newe Bedsteede withe a halfe hea[d] at his choice". To Alice a round table board which his daughter Joan Cicill is to keep until Alice shall "have neede thereof".

Residue equally divided between son John and daughter Joan, executors.

Witnesses: John Harris, shoemaker, and his wife; Nicholas Chambers, parish clerk of St. Philip's, [and others].

n.b. After its transcription by the Extra Mural Class the condition of this will deteriorated, and parts of the text were lost; it has since been repaired. Sections which survive only in transcription are shown in [ ].

57 ROGER COOK, tanner, [St. Philip], 12 December 1597.

Soul to almighty God "my maker And Redeamere, And my Bodye to the yerthe from whence yt Came to be Layde in christian Byriall by my father in Sainte Phillipes churche". 20s apiece to John Durnell his 3 (daughters *deleted*) children. To [Thomas*] Lewis "my man" 40s. To the hospital £5.

Residue, debts, legacies and funeral charges being paid, to wife Elizabeth, sole executrix.

Overseer: Mathew Cable to whom 10s for his pains.

Witnesses: William Wyett, whittawer, Evan Morgan, tanner, Lewis Prichard, Evan Morgan [*see above; this second entry was clearly made in error and is marked* NEM' *(no-one)*]

[Note in Latin to the effect that executrix sworn in on 24 December 1597 in person of Thomas Prin,Notary Public. Note on another copy of the will that inventory exhibited 18 February 1597/8 noting £142 16s 2d in goods and £131 6s 8d in debts. The name marked* was omitted in copy will.]

58 RALPH CORNISH, tailor, Christchurch, 26 September 1597, proved 1 October 1597.

Soul to almighty God, body to be buried in Christian burial at discretion of executrix.

To brother Harry 20 nobles to be delivered within three months of his decease to William Watson and Thomas Marten, overseers, to have the use of the money during Harry's apprenticeship, "they yeldinge after the rate of viijli in the hundreth, and putting in sureties to the chamber of Bristoll for the payment thereof togeather with the said increase at the time afore limitted which is and shalbe within two yeares after the end of his said prenticeshippe and not afore".

To brother William his violet cloak, his best hat and best doublet, his best band and best shirt. To William Watson, overseer, his second piece of rug, next to the biggest. To Thomas Marten, overseer, the "least peace of Rugge". To John Smythe his partner the biggest piece of rug, "all which peaces are in my shoppe".

To the poor of Christchurch 10s to be distributed in bread. To the poor of St. James 10s to be distributed in bread. To his maidservant Christian Downe 5s.

Residue to wife Alice, sole executrix.

Witnesses: "me Morgan Jones the writer hereof and Thomas Marten".

59   JOHN COULTON, whittawer, [?St. James], 21 October 1597, proved 10 November 1597

Sick in body. Soul into God's hands, body to be laid "in the yearthe the mother of all fleshe". Walter Chester of Bristol, gent., and Christopher Conwaye, carpenter, bound to testator in £12; they are to be discharged. Executrix to pay testator's debt of £4 14s to his sister's daughter Anne Coulton. To wife Katherine £5 for meat, drink, linen, woollen and all things necessary for his mother Agnes Coulton; if she refuses, £5 to said mother.

Residue, debts and funeral discharged, to wife Katherine, sole executrix.

Overseers: Mr. Thomas Parker and Thomas Corye to whom 12d apiece for their pains.

All testator's clothes to kinsman William Coulton.

Witnesses: Robert Dower, Thomas Newton and William Coulton.

Debts owed by testator:
to Thomas Parker between £16 and £18
of receipts to the Company of Whittawers for which John Howlett stands bound £17
more he received £4 13s 4d
received in rent of John Ho[wle]tt 20s
in account to John Howlett for the Company's breakfast 8s 8d
to Mr. John Dowle £4

Debts owing to testator:
Mr. Vicar Coulman owes 2s 4d
John James owes 20s
he stands bound for John James to Mr. Gryffen 25s
one Bufforde a carpenter upon a bond together with Robert Parsons £4

60 KATHERINE COULTON, widow, St. James, 1 December 1597, proved 12 December 1597.

Soul to almighty God, body to be buried in Christian burial.

To son John Roome £10 and a feather bed. To sister Elizabeth Morse all her apparel both linen and woollen, and two pillows with pillow-beres.

To apprentices Robert Dower and George Crompe a little crock and a charger each. To Judith Williams a half headed bedstead.

To poor of St. James' parish 3s 4d to be distributed at discretion of executor.

Residue to son Edward Roome, sole executor, revoking all former wills.

Overseers: Christopher Conwaye, John Howlett, each to have 6d.

Witnesses: "Morgan Jones the writer hereof", Thomas Langley, John Howllet, Christopher Conwaye.

61 THOMAS DOLE, yeoman, [St. Peter], 10 April 1597, proved 4 June 1597.

Being weak of body; soul to "god the Father of heaven my Creator, and to Jhesus Christ my Redeemer and to god the hollie ghost my comforter . . . trusting to be saved and my synnes pardoned by the precious blood Death and merits onlie of Jhesus Christ." To be buried in St Peter's church at pew door "of my good Mother" or where she thinks good; 6s 8d for the ground. To Mr Thomas James parson of the said parish 3s 4d. To the poor of the parish 20s whereof 6s 8d to the poorest prisoners of Newgate.

Mother to enjoy for life messuage where she now dwells "as one woorthie of more lardg interrest thereof"; after her death —— testator's youngest brother to enjoy it for life provided mother allows to be paid by William Dole junior —— £20 towards these debts: to Thomas Tailor of Bristol, grocer £10; to Richard Boswell apothecary £3 6 8d; to brother William Dole the elder towards discharge of a debt which executors of Peter M——w deceased challenge £6 13 4d.

Aforesaid house to brother William Dole the elder and his heirs after death of mother Joan and brother William the younger; brother William the elder to have "evidences and writinges" concerning the house after mother's death; for lack of heirs of William the elder, to brother Richard Dole now in Ireland and his heirs; for lack of issue to William Dole the younger and his heirs for ever. To said brother —— term of years unexpired of new dwelling house over against St Peter's Cross —— provided the best wainscot —— and testator's square wainscot table to be delivered to cousin —— Flower; to said cousin Alice testator's part of Vane L—— er's debt which mother freely gave testator, to be yielded to her immediately upon the recovery by law.

—— house in Wine Street now in occupation of George Mo(m)ford glover within one year by mother's consent to be —— to pay £20 to be distributed as follows: to [sister Joan Fagott] cloth 40s; to brother-in-law Thomas Fagott to be converted into a gold ring 40s; to sister Elizabeth Parker 20s and brother-in-law Thomas Parker 20s. To cousin Susan Gr——onney £5. "I owe hereby a larger considderacion." To Elizabeth Griffith testator's god daughter being the natural daughter ——cousin Susan 40s; to goodwife Wiggins £2 10s; to Robert Amtill barber —— to Robert Woofford 40s and all testator's apparel; to Jane wife of Peter Reade 6s 8d; to ——llyn his mother's servant 3s 4d which particular sums with money for the grave and Mr James and the poor amount to £20 to be paid from tenement in occupation of George Momford.

To Mrs Wickham, widow, in Wine Street "my good frend" his small spruce chest to be delivered by William Dole ——; to brother William Dole the elder "my dagger which latelie he gave unto me".

William Dole the elder sole executor; overseers brothers-in-law Thomas Fagott and Thomas Parker. Written "with my owne hand and in my howsse at Sainct——"; delivered to Thomas Fagott " to be forth commyng ymediatlie after my discease which he Receaved of me the xi th of April Anno 1597".

Witnesses: Robert Woford, William Bysshop.

62 ROBERT FREWELL, Bristol, 29 August 1597, inventory exhibited 17 December 1597. [endorsement "Att Cadbery the fyrst of Septmber 1597"].

Appoints wife Edith sole executrix, revoking all former wills.

Witnesses: goodwife Edwards, goodwife Jonnes, and "others with his sister", Richard Kelke.

63 WILLIAM HANBYE, freemason, St. Philip, 4 April 1597, proved 9 April 1597.

Sick in body; "I comend my Soule to almyghtie god the maker and redeemer therof" and body to be buried in St. Philip's churchyard. To son William one bedstead being in the back chamber with one flock-bed, one pair of sheets, one coverlet and one bolster.

To daughter Margaret one half-head bedstead with a tester of stained cloth being in the fore chamber and one brass candlestick, one platter and one pottinger.

Residue to wife Joan, executrix.

Witnesses: John Settell, Thomas Watts and Anthony Frinde with others.

Debts due to testator:
Mr. Gorge dwelling at "Michaelhill" [St. Michael's Hill] 22s 6d
Simon Batten for 3 loads of Dundry stone taken from Redcliffe Hill 15s 9d
"more he owethe me for worcke" 14s 6d

Oliver Mockett freemason, owes for work 39s
"he oweth me for one loade of stones" 5s 3d
Sum of debts: £4 17s

Debts owed by testator:
to Richard Checke 6s 8d
to Robert Elson 2s
Sum: 8s 8d

64 MAURICE HULL alias HILL, St. Philip, 11 June 1597, proved
1597

Soul to the holy Trinity, "most stedfastly beleeving that mi salvacion
restethe onlie in mi saviour Jesus Christ, through his death and passion,
and by no other meanes". Body to Christian burial in St. James, "as neare
my first wiffe as convenientli mey be".
    To his "trustie lovinge frend Edward Baker of Tockington . . . yeoman"
all rents and profits from his lands and tenements in Tockington and
Aucley, and in the marsh in Tockington parish, and in Almondsbury
parish, except one piece of ground called Stapleyn about 15 acres, to
remain to his son Walter towards his education.
    The rents and profits of the rest of his lands and tenements to Edward
Baker, towards payment of testator's debts. Edward Baker to pay testator's daughter Cicely £100 at 18 years, "yf she match by the consent of
her frendes or otherwisse at her full age of Twentie and one yeares".
    To Edward Baker 40s annually out of the profits of his lands and tene-
ments "towardes his paines" over and above all necessary charges
incurred in executing the will, "and for the residue he to be counteable
unto my said sonne Walter of all receiptes and paymentes". This to be
delivered within a month of the end of the year to the Chamberlain of
Bristol, to the use of son Walter, he to have the benefit after the rate of £8
in the hundred.
    To son Thomas an annuity of £20 from the age of 21. Edward Baker to
pay £5 annually towards the education and bringing up of Thomas.
    To poor of St. Philip's parish 10s. To poor of St. James' parish 10s.
Another 10s to be distributed at the discretion of his overseers, where
most needed.
    Son Walter sole executor.

Overseers: Edward Bosden, William Birde, gents. of Bristol.

Note that testator borrowed £60 from Maurice Tovie of Thornbury, giving
as surety a deed of feoffment of lands in Tockington, near Walney. The
£60 has been repaid by testator, but Maurice Tovie has not returned deeds.
Witnesses of repayment: old Thomas Pryer of Olveston, John Smith of
West Streete, John Burrnell of "the Bannet tree", also Thomas Prin and
James Cleate his servants.

65 JOHN HUNT, tanner, [St. Peter], 3 June 1597, proved 1 July 1597.

Sick in body and "consideringe the mutabylitie & uncertainty of this transitorie world" bequeaths soul to almighty God "who hath Created & redeemed me and all the world"; body to be buried in St. Peter's churchyard.
  Debts to be paid if any appear by writing, bill, score or sufficient record. To the poor 6s 8d.
  To legitimate son Hugh Hunt £6 13s 4d at age of 21 years and to legitimate daughter Agnes Hunt £6 13d 4d at day of marriage; if either die, the other to receive that portion or if both die, wife Agnes to enjoy both portions.
  Residue to wife Agnes Hunte, sole executrix "whome also I desire to be Lovinge and frindlie to my children & to see them browghte up in the feare & nurture of the Lord".

Overseers: brother Joseph Hunte and brother-in-law Nicholas Addams to whom 12d each for a token. The mark of John Hunte.

Witnesses: Nicholas Addams, James Farley, Thomas Phelps, William Hunt.

Codicil 4 June [1597] to children Hugh and Agnes 6 sheep to be equally divided between them and the increase and profit thereof to be employed to their use and benefit.

66 ELIZABETH JONES, widow, St. Mary Redcliffe, nuncupative, 2 May 1597, proved 23 July 1597.

To Margaret Tilley of Lieghe a napkin. To Margaret's son 1s.
  Residue to Elizabeth Rogers of Bristol, widow, sole executrix, also all debts owed to testatrix.

Overseers: William Vowles, John Owen, sen. each to have 6d.

Witnesses: Clement Barnes, William Dabes, Nicholas Dabes, William Vowles.

67 MARGARET JOONS, widow, [St. Thomas], (23 November 1597).

Testatrix's debts 23 November 1597:
to Margery 10s
to Mistress Pr[e]wett 8s
to Mary Hill 2s
to Robert Stevens 3s 9d
to Richard Stevens 3s 4d
to "bucher the collier" 3s
to John Cooke 1s 4d
to Richard Lentorn 1s
to Robert Humphery 4s

Sick of body. Soul "to the hands of god my creator & to Jesus Christ my savior." To be buried in the churchyard of St. Thomas.

Executrix Alice Maisy her servant.

Overseers: John Grigg and Thomas Prestwod.

Memorandum: "William Weall hath a Ceverlett in pane [pawn] for v s"

68 JOHN KNIGHT, vicar of All Saints, 31 May 1597, proved July 23 1597.

Soul into the hands of God, "as unto my faithfull Creator and to Jesus Christ my onelie saviour and redeemer and hoping to be saved by his most pretious death and passion and by no meritte or deserts of myne; and fullie affirming my self that throughe beleefe in him I shall obteyne remission of my sinnes and all other benefites of his passion". Body to be buried in chancel of All Saints church.

"The portion of goods which god hath lent unto me I give and bequeath them as followeth":

To his father-in-law Robert Estope alias White all his working tools and a dagger knife. To his sister Christian 10s.

To Thomas Kedgwyn, Martinius Hebrew Grammar, to John Atkins, minister, "Daneus upon the small Prophetts which he hath" and his crooked sword.

To William Hulyn, "Henry Smithes sermon in quarto", to Mr. Marten "Vicker of Temple, so many bookes as I have of Piscator's woorkes".

To Mr Durant of St. Werburgh, two books, "Marlorat uppon Mathew and John". To Mr. Gulliford "Gwalter upon the small Prophetts". To Mr Richard Pettingale "the booke he hath of mine in his custodie". To Mr. Woodson all his books of physic or surgery, to Mr. Hollinster, Lodewick Lloyd's chronicles and "the enemie of securitie guilt".

To Mr. Alderman Cole "Besaes testament in lardg quarto with Psalmes". To William Sherman, Bullinger's decades in English in quarto. To Mrs. Colston Foxes Prayers. To Mr. Richard Dyer and Mr. William Robinson, ministers and preachers of the word of God, all the rest of his books, except his great study Bible, bequeathed to his wife.

Richard Dyer and William Robinson to pay testator's debts to the value of £10, if any residue of the £10 remain after funeral expenses and debts are paid, this to go to his wife.

All his notebooks, paper books and loose papers to Mr. William Robinson.

Residue to wife, sole executrix.

Overseers: Mr. Edward Hollinster and Robert Estope alias White.

Witnesses: William Robinson, William Shermond.

69   THOMAS MOWREY, tailor, St. Nicholas, 3 December 1597, proved 19 January 1597/8.

Sick in body. Soul into the hands of "God my creator and —— Christ my redeemer hoping to be saved by his meritts and death of —— same my saviour Christ through faith in his blood".

To wife Elizabeth, sole executrix, "the small po[rtion of] goods which god hath in mercie bestowed uppon me".

Witnesses: William Robinson, vicar of St. Nicholas, Nicholas Crundall.

70   CICELY NAYLER, widow, St. Stephen, 22 August 1597, proved 19 October 1597.

Soul to almighty God, "my creator and redeemer assuredlye trustinge by faithe in Jesus Christe my saviour to inherrite the heavenly kingedome". Body to be buried in the parish church.

To Anne Hedges her daughter £10, "to be made out of my goods into monye", to be given by executrix to Thomas Addams, overseer, to keep for 4 years. If Anne die before 4 years expires then £10 to be divided equally between her 2 children.

To the 2 children of Anne Hedges £10, to be made from sale of testatrix's goods and divided equally between them, and given on reaching 21 years. If either die before this then that portion to go to the other. If both die before 21 years the whole to go to executrix.

To her sister Jane Spanne of Chepstow her best gown, a feather bed, a feather bolster, 2 pairs of sheets and a coverlet of Irish "rugge". To Jane Spanne's 2 daughters Ursula and Joan, 3 platters, a flock bed and bolster, a pair of sheets and a coverlet of "rugge" each.

To George Bonnde, her brother's son, a feather bed with bolster, a pair of sheets and a rug, to be delivered at the "adge of xxjtie yeares". To his brother Thomas Bonnde a flock bed with bolster, a rug and a pair of sheets, to be delivered at 21 years. If either die first then bequests to remain to executrix. To the 6 daughters of her brother Bonnde 5s each.

To daughter Anne her gilt wine bowl. To god daughter Anne Addams a bed of half feathers and half flock with bolster, a pair of sheets and a rug. To Joan Worley his daughter 20s when she becomes 21. If she die first bequest to remain to executrix. To Katherine Howell a flock bed and bolster, a pair of sheets, a platter and a crock.

To cousin Julian George her best smock. To Elizabeth Hedges a flock bed and bolster, a pair of sheets, a rug and 2 platters. To James Webbe her apprentice a flock bed, a bolster, a pair of sheets, a rug, a bedstead and a chest, "and do forgeve his covenannte yeare which he hathe to serve withall his benefitt and profitt of that yeare and of his viadge savinge only his wage[e] . . . of his viadge".

To the Master and Company of "the Whoopers" 10s to drink on the day of her funeral. To Nicholas Hedges 4 silver spoons, and to his brother John Hedges a silver salt. To god daughter Joan Phillipps 20s to be kept by overseer Thomas Addams until she reach 21 years; if she die first then bequest to remain to executrix.

40s to be distributed in bread to the poor on the day of her funeral. To Goodwife Braye of the almshouse 4d every Sunday for life.

Residue to daughter Anne Hedges, sole executrix.

Overseers: Thomas Addams of Bristol, ropemaker, and John Clarke, vintner, to have 10s each.

Witnesses: Thomas Addams, John Clarke, John Barnatt, William Atkins, Daniel Addams and John Davis, notary public.

71   EDWARD NICHOLLS, St. Thomas, 16 June 1597, proved 1 August 1597.

Sick in body. Soul to "god my creator trustinge to be saved by the deathe & passion of Christ Jesus my only redeemer"; body to be buried in the churchyard of St. Thomas.

To eldest son Edward at 21 years one tenement in the market place of Ross in the tenure of Richard Underwood, with garden adjoining. To second son Richard at 21 years "my other tenement" adjoining the bell-forge in Ross with a garden in Ederosse St. If either son die under 21, testator's youngest son Walter to have the tenement. If all his sons die without issue the tenements are to remain to his daughters Agnes and Elizabeth.

To son Walter £20 at age 21. If through the death of either of his brothers he shall enjoy either of the said tenements, then £10 of the money bequeathed to him to be divided between testator's 2 daughters.

To daughter Agnes £20 at age 21 or "yf she marry before at the day of her mariage by her mothers discretion". To younger daughter Elizabeth £20 in same manner as aforesaid. To poor of St. Thomas 5s.

Residue to wife Katherine, executrix.

Overseers: John Slye and Giles Goughe.

Witnesses: Samuel Davis, preacher, John Slye, Giles Goughe with others. [A note that the following was endorsed (*retro script*) indicates that this is a copy; there is also a note that this will was proved in the P.C.C., London.]

Best black cloak to brother Walter Nicholls and next best cloak to brother Thomas Nicholls; to brother Haggar "myother blacke cloake" and "unto my sister Elizabethe Haggar a mourninge gowne".

72   MARY OLFYLDE, singlewoman, Christchurch, 27 September 1597, nuncupative, proved 29 October, 1597.

To her sister Maud Tyther's 5 children £10, that is 40s each, and to Maud Tyther £3. To her sister Anne Graunte £3. To her brother John Olfylde £3. 20s to be laid out on her burial, "which £20 she said was in the hands of her brother in lawe Thomas Tyther late deceased".

Witness: Anne Butcher, wife of John Butcher late sheriff of Bristol.

73   EDMUND POPLEY, ironmonger, [Christchurch], 9 June 1597, proved 25 August 1597

Sick in body. Soul "into the hands of god my maker to Jesus Christ my redeemer & to the holy ghost my sanctifier hoping to be saved by the meritts and mercies deathe and passion of Jesus Christ and to enioye that everlasting kingdom prepared for the faithfull". Body to the earth in Christchurch churchyard "untill the greate day of resurreccion of the just."
   To son Edmund £40 and to son Derrick (Diricke) £50, at age 25. To daughter Anne £50 at the day of her marriage. To Edmund one salt with a cover both silver gilt and a stone pot covered with silver and "one ring of gould with my name uppon it" which he shall receive at age 25. To son Derrick "my fairest guilt boule" and one stone pot covered with silver. To daughter Anne another gilt bowl and one stone pot covered with silver; all this plate to be delivered after death of wife Joan. £5 to be given (20s apiece) to sister Eaton's 5 children.
   To preachers of the word of God Mr Robert Gulliford 40s, Mr John Pittes 20s and William Robinson 20s. To John [Grigg*] clerk of St. Nicholas, 10s. To the poor at the time of testator's burial 40s. To his apprentice John Macey 10s "using himselfe well & honestly towards my wiffe & not otherwise". To servant Elizabeth Bayley 10s "if she behave herselfe well & honestly also towards my wiffe".
   Residue to wife Joan "whole executrix."

Overseers: William Dyeos and Thomas Clement to whom 20s each.

[Witnesses: William Robinson, vicar of St. Nicholas, William Deyos, grocer, Anthony Hill, grocer, Bartholomew Hill.*]

[*The bottom of the will is damaged but missing portions marked * have been supplied from a copy of the will recorded in the Great Orphan Book.*]

74   JOHN POWELL, shoemaker, St. Peter, 6 June 1597, proved 6 August 1597.

Soul into the hands of God, "my creator assuringe my selffe to be saved and to Inheryt the Joyes prepared for the Ellect through the myrittes and blood sheedinge of Jesus Christe my onlye saviour and redeemer". Body to be buried in St. Peter's church, "as neare unto my pewe doore as maye be".

To Ellen Trule his maidservant 40s.

To the poor of St. Peters's 10s to be distributed at discretion of overseers.

To wife Auberry, remainder of the lease of his house in Broad Street, so long as she remains unmarried, but "after her marriadge or howre of deathe" the residue of years to Walter Powell his son.

To his mother 20s to be paid quarterly fo life. To son Walter all his apparel.

Residue to wife Auberry, sole executrix, "she to see me decently brought to the earthe".

Overseers: Mr. Richard Smithe, William Wyatt.

Witnesses: Mr. Richard Smithe, Mr. Robert Flower.

75 THOMAS RIDER, clerk, Redcliffe (Recklie), 25 April 1597, proved 26 June 1597.

Sick in body. Soul "to allmigtie god my onlie maker and redemer".

To son William Ridder all testator's wearing apparel, books and his bow and arrows. Residue to wife Alice, sole executrix.

Witnesses : William Ridder his son, William Inwode and Eleanor Inwode his wife.

76 THOMAS ROGERS, Temple, 30 May 1597, proved 9 July 1597.

"Thomas Regeres off the parres of Tempolle beyn syke yn bode and holle yn mynde do macke my laste wylle and testamentte I be quethe my sowlle to allemeyghtty God and my bode to the yerthe and I geve and be quethe to Welsyon my wiffe alle my goodes movabolle and omovabolle botte and yff my wyffe do chance here afftte to marry wth any man thatt Wyllyam Cox and James Belleman beyn my ower sseares shalle notte leke welle off hyme thatt then the to howsses wyche she have shalle Remayne to the yowsse off my sone edewarde and to brynge hyme oppe to skolle and to lernyn on tylle he be a bolle to be potte to ssome ockapassyon alleso I geve to my Sone John Regeres iiii chelderyn iis a pece off theme to be payde theme att my [laste end off my lyffe *deleted*] [—e of iiii yeres *inserted but partially blotted*] I geve to my cusson Thomas Coutes alle my warren parrelle saven my beste gone to Remayne to my wyffe.

Wretten to be wyttenes yn the Pressence off Thomas Gebebe and John Everette".

77   JOAN SYMONS, widow, St. Ewen (Audoens), 5 September 1597, proved 25 October 1597.

Widow of Thomas Symons late of the City of Bristol, merchant, deceased.

Soul "into the handes of almighty god stedfastly beleving to be saved by the precious death and passion of his sone Jesus Christe my most lovinge saviour and redeemer".

Body to be buried at discretion of son Thomas Symons, sole executor, to whom she leaves all her goods and chattels.

78   JOHN VEYSEY, tailor, St. Peter, 30 September 1597, proved 29 October 1597.

Soul to almighty God, body to be buried in St. Peter's churchyard, "as neare to my children as maybe".

To Joyce Veysey his eldest daughter the flock bed in the upper loft and a bolster, a pair of sheets, a platter, a pottinger, and a saucer. To Goodlove Veysey his daughter his ⸺ crock save [one], [*will damaged*], a pair of sheets, a platter, a pottinger, a saucer and a candlestick. To Pascae Veysey his son the biggest kettle, a pair of sheets, a platter, a pottinger, a saucer and a candlestick.

Residue to wife Joan, sole executrix.

Witnesses: Thomas James, parson, Eleanor Abbinton with others.

79   JOHN VINCENT, St. Thomas, 20 June 1597, proved 30 July 1597.

Being "sick and weake in bodie"; soul to God and body to be buried at discretion of executrix.

All goods and chattels to wife Christian, sole executrix.

Witnesses: Thomas Callowhill, John James, James Cadell.

80   ELIZABETH WAKER, widow, St. Mary le Port, 26 April 1597, admon. 4 June 1597.

Soul into the hands of God, body to be buried in St. Mary le Port churchyard.

To wife of John Hopttan, cutler, of St. Peter's parish, her "grogrem" gown, her best red petticoat, best kerchief, best partlet, best pillow, and wooden chair.

Residue to William Higges, shoemaker, of St. Mary Port Street, he to see her buried in the place where William Dason was buried.

Witnesses: Mistress Hart in St. Mary Port Street, Christopher Herison, hosier, and Humphrey Grymmer, shoemaker.

81 RICHARD WESTACOTT, Bristol, mariner, 12 December 1596, proved 16 December 1597.

Soul to almighty God, maker and redeemer; body to the earth.

To his children Mary and Susan, the moiety or "halfendeale" of all his goods. If one of them should die before age 21 or marry, then her part to go to the other one. The other moiety to wife Elizabeth, executrix.

Witnesses: Peter Punchard, Robert Westcotes, George Long. [Written by Peter Punchard].

82 PETER WHITEHEAD, yeoman, St. Philip, 21 March 1596/7, proved 9 April 1597.

Soul to almighty God, body to be buried in St. Philip's churchyard.

To Elizabeth Dukes his servant his second best bed and bedstead, a bolster, a pair of sheets, 2 blankets, his iron crock, 2 platters, a frieze (frice) gown and a red petticoat.

To Elizabeth Parson his cousin a cloth petticoat, a flannel petticoat, a linen smock, his russet cloak, a pair of stockings, a pair of shoes, a partlet, a kerchief and a head napkin.

Residue to John Horsey of Bristol, sailor, and Robert Craftesman, his two kinsmen, equally divided.

Overseers: Mr. Thomas Colman, vicar of St. Philip's, and Arthur Panthur of Bristol.

Witnesses: Mr. Colman, Arthur Panthur and Nicholas Chambers, parish clerk.

83 ELIZABETH WILLIAMS, widow, St. Peter, 25 August 1597, proved 3 September 1597.

Sick in body. Soul to almighty god, creator and redeemer in whom she trusts to be saved "and by non other". To be buried in St. Peter's church as near her husband as possible. Bequest —— for breaking the ground, making the grave and laying the stone.

To the poor of St. Peter's parish 5s to be distributed by Mr. James "our parson". To "the clarke a —— ringers to ring for me" 5s. Parson Mr. T[homas] James to read "orderly servis" at her burial, 10s for his pains plus a pair of breeches and a cassock without sleeves to make him a coat. To 4 men that have been wardens of the company of the pointmakers to carry her to church and lay her in the grave 6s. To the masters of the pointmakers to drink 6s. To the poor 10s "to b——ed in bread and to be dystributed by my overseers".

To Catherine Warren, eldest daughter of John Warren, a great candle-stick, "my spewse cheste", the board cupboard and half a dozen stools, a chair, a —— ery full and wholly as it stands in the lower hall, "my furnis" and great brandiron, two pairs of she—— and " a shorte", a dozen of nap-kins, one half of one sort and the other half of another sort, a —— oyders. To Alice Warren a candlestick, a charger, the biggest crock, a pair of sh ——, a dozen of napkins, the biggest pair of pothooks, the biggest broach (broche) and the biggest pair of andirons, —— "voyders".

To Joan Hamons "my lesser fether bed and lesser bolster", the middle crock, a pair of po——, a skimmer, a dripping pan, the great chest, a chaf-ing -dish, a pair of sheets, a table cloth, a pillow, 3 b—— ches, a pillow-bere, 3 platters, 3 pottingers, 2 voiders, a candlestick. To Jane Warde the —— save one, the stained cloths in the hall, 20s in money, "a pott tellpote ", 2 long towels, a coverlet, a bolster, a kett—— down pillow, a candle-stick,a spice mortar, a present pint pot, a board, a bedstead, a pair of sheets, 3 platters, —— saucers, 3 pottingers, a new piece of cloth.

To Joan Anuley "my beste fetherbed, my beste bolster my best —— ", a square board, a gold ring, the stained cloths in the upper hall, a candle-stick, 2 flower pots and a new su—— . To Alice Langley "my best cas-socke", the stained cloths in the chamber "where I lye and ij cupes of tynn —— bedstead I lie in", a quart pot, a candlestick, 2 "poynte pots", 2 old candlesticks, 2 flower pots, a gold ring, a —— smock. To Eleanor Abbinton "the bed I lye on", the red coverlet, a strong pair of sheets, —— old pan, a towel, the bedstead in the cockloft and 3s in money. To Margaret Brian the truckle [bed] in the chamber and the bed and bolster upon it, a towel, a —— sheets and a coverlet.

To "poore Joa —— [some]tyme beinge my servant, my old pettycote and olde cassocke." To the 4 children born of Alice W—— 5s each. To —— James 2 platters, a pottinger, a pint pot, a quart pot, 3 flower pots. To Edmund Anewley —— chair in the hall and the limbeck with the "[?p]ypes". To Henry Langley a chair.

Residue to Catherine Warren, Alice Warren and Joan Hamons whom she makes executors.

Overseers: Thomas James "our parson" and Ralph Thom—— to whom 4s each.

Witnesses: Alice Langley, ——, Margaret Brian and others.

Proved before Samuel Davys.

84   MARGARET YOUNGE, widow, Christchurch, 6 March 1596/7, proved 30 March 1597.

Soul into the hands of God, body to be buried in Christchurch.

To Edith Palmer, daughter of her brother James Palmer, a chest or cof-fer, and 40s to be paid on her marriage. To Elizabeth Palmer her sister a chest or coffer and 40s to be paid on her marriage. To Elizabeth Cripps, daughter of testatrix's daughter Elizabeth Pollington, a gold ring value 10s.

To 10 poor women a gown of frieze and a kerchief each "to go with me to my buriall".

Testatrix's daughter Joyce Yeoman, "whole" executrix.

Overseers: William Yeoman and Giles Goughe.

Witnesses: William Yeoman, Giles Goughe, Susan Northall and Alice Morgan.

85   ROBERT BURGES, butcher, St. Thomas, 2 February 1598/9, proved 3 March 1598/9.

Sick of body; soul into the hands of almighty God, saviour and redeemer and body to the earth. To son John Burges £6 13s 4d. To the child "that my wife now goeth withall" £6 13s 4d, " to be paid unto everie of them" at 21 years; overseers to put out children's legacy for the best advantage of his children.

To mother Joan Burges £5 at next Whitsuntide; to sister Alice Burges £4 of which 52s is a debt of his to her, to be paid next Easter. To the poor of St. Thomas parish 3s 4d. To the Minister of St Thomas, James Listun, 3s 4d. If either of his two children die before age 21, his portion to remain to the other.

Residue to wife Ursula, whole executor.

Overseers: "welbeloved in Christ" William Priddie and John Stibbins, to whom 10s each.

Witnesses: John Stibbins, Thomas Cliff, James Listun, curate of St. Thomas.

Debts due to testator:
John Pope of East Dundry for a steer 20s
old father Danniell of Whitchurch for a quarter of beef 14s 10d
James Barbour owes for two beasts meat 6s
Debts testator owes:
To Thomas Cliffe £4 6s to be paid at 1s weekly.
To John Stibbins £3 6s 3/4d as it appears on a score
To the bailiff of Bedminster 9s
To William Danniell "of St. Johns wood that keepes my cattle" 6s
To James Barbour 2 dozen skins of calves as appears on a score.
His cattle in sundry places:
in "St Jones woode and in shorte woode" 16 hard beasts, 4 yearlings, 22 sheep and a gray nag.
"Item more with my mother-in-law a cowpple of pigs".

Memorandum that he paid £4 to one Thomas Day of Whitchurch whose son-in-law Whippie was witness at John Richmond's house, for piece of ground of 9 acres called "shortwoode" lying by "St Joanes woode" for one year from 1 March next being "St. Davies daie".

86   SAMPSON BURGES, Redcliffe, 12 November 1597, proved 3 August 1598.

Soul to almighty God, his saviour and redeemer, body to the earth.

To daughter Anne Burges £5 and his best bible, a "great brasse catheren" and a charger, to be given within a year of his decease to his overseers, to her use. If his wife Margaret marry within that year, then legacy to be given on her marriage as above.

To daughter Prudence Burges £5, a great crock, his old bible and a charger, to be given on same terms as above. To daughter Joan Burges £6 and a charger, on same terms.

If any of his daughters die before receiving their legacy, it to be divided among the survivors. If all three die before receiving their legacies then these to remain to wife Margaret.

To brother Richard Burges his best rug gown.

Residue to wife, sole executrix.

Overseers: brother-in-law Robert Weale and brother Richard Burges.

Witnesses: Thomas Wathen and Richard Burges.

87   JOAN BURNETT, widow, Bristol, admon. granted 21 October 1598.

Late wife of William Burnett of the said city, cardmaker; gives all her goods to William Edwardes of the said city, cardmaker, on condition he "shall tende mee and find mee meate and drinke and all thinges necessary duringe my lief and when it shall please god to call me" William to see her buried, pay her debts and discharge her funeral.

Mark of Joan Burnett

Witnesses: Thomas Puxston and William Yeamans; mark of Thomas Cicill.

88   RICHARD COOPER, clothier, Temple, 13 November 1598, proved 16 December 1598.

Soul to almighty God, his maker, redeemer and sanctifier, body to be buried in the chancel of Temple church, "to rest tyll it shall please god to raise it upp to the resurrection in the life everlasting".

To the poor of Temple parish 10s to be distributed on the day of his funeral.

To daughter Anne Cooper £20 to be paid at the age of 21 years, or her marriage, whichever is first.

Overseers: William ?Chaundler of Temple parish and James Taylor, each to have 5s.

To Richard Martin, vicar of Temple church, 5s.

Residue to wife Anne, sole executrix.

All former wills, testaments, legacies, executors and overseers revoked.

Joan daughter of "my predissessor Thomas Perkin" to receive of testator's wife £20 at her marriage or when she reach 21 years, according to a covenant made between testator and his wife before they were married.

Witnesses: Richard Martine, Richard Balye and William Morgan.

89   EDMOND EDWARDS, baker, St. Thomas 13 April 1598, proved 21 April 1598.

Sick of body; soul into the hands of almighty God, maker, redeemer and saviour. Body to be buried in the chancel of Temple church "as nighe my mother as may be, there to remain till God shall raise it up in the glorious resurrection of life everlastinge."

To poor of Temple parish 40s to be distributed at his funeral, of which 20s to be given in bread and the other 20s in ready money. To Richard Martin, vicar of Temple, in satisfaction for grave and other demands "my spice dishe which my grandmother gave me in her last will, it waeghes an eleaven ounzes."

To father Sampson Edwards "my best goblet with the cover pertayninge thereunto, and my best tankard" and £5 money presently after decease. Said father to have £21 of the money Thomas Brooke is to pay testator, which money is to be paid to William Packer of the city of Bristol 17th April, for which sum father is bound.

Residue to wife Denise (Dennys), executrix.

Overseers: his father Sampson Edwards and John Sanfflocke, of Warminster (Warmester) yeoman; 10s to said John. Revokes former wills.

Mark of Edward Edwards.

Witnesses: Richard Martine, vicar of Temple, Thomas Callowhill, [?] J. Sayer, William Alford, Thomas Brooke.

90   THEOPHILUS FLETCHER, gent., late of London, now of Bristol, 20 March 1598/9, proved 1598/9.

"beinge now bound for Irelande and fully determined to serve her majestie in her warres there, and for that I know there is nothinge more certen than death, and then the time and place . . . nothing more uncerten, I do therefore ordaine and make this my last will amd testament in manner and forme followinge."

Soul into the hands of almighty God, and Jesus Christ "my redeemer, by whose most precious death and blood shedd I only [tr]ust to be savede", body to the earth "where soever it shall please god to give it buriall".

To brothers and sisters, Nathaniel, John, Sarah, Phoebe and Mary Fletcher, 20s each to buy a ring, to wear for his sake.

To uncles Dr. Fletcher of London and Mr. Pownoll of Bristol, 20s each to buy a ring, to wear for his remembrance.

To his Aunt Pownoll of Bristol, 40s to buy a ring, to wear for his sake.

To sister Priscilla Fletcher, £5 "to be bestowed upon some prittie jewell", to wear for his sake.

Residue to sister Elizabeth Fletcher, sole executrix.

All former wills revoked.

Covenant with executrix to pay her 100 marks if he nullifies present will without her consent in writing.

Overseer: "my most lovinge and kinde unckle Mr. Pownoll of Bristol" to have 20s over and above his legacy.

Witnesses: Israel Gleson, notary public, Nathaniel Pownoll, notary public, John Whitakorn, scribe.

91   ROBERT GARRETT, St. Peter, 4 October 1598, proved 4 November 1598.

Sick in body; soul to almighty God, creator and redeemer and "in him I truste to be saved and by non other". Body to be buried in the churchyard of St. Peter's.

To daughter Alice Garrett white rug (roudge) coverlet, a pair of hurden sheets, 2 chargers, a platter, a pottinger, 2 little kettles and a coffer "rygoled". To daughter Elizabeth Garrett "the bydger bolster", a pair of hurden sheets, 3 platters, one old bed, the biggest cathern and a little cathern and a new coffer; his children to have their portions at 21 years, portion of any dying before coming of age to go to other.

Residue to wife Agnes, executrix.

Overseer: Robert Benett.

Witnesses: Thomas James, clerk and others.

To "my brother" John Jones best doublet and leather breeches.

Proved before the Chancellor.

92   THOMAS GOODMAN, Bristol, 10 April 1598, proved 24 October 1598.

Soul to almighty God, body to the earth.

To Maud Goodman his wife a flock bed, a bolster, a white coverlet, ―――― sheets, [*will damaged*], and the bedstead he lies in, a brass crock, a platter, a "pochenger", a saucer, a salt cellar, a candlestick, all her apparel, a coffer with a spring lock "wherein she do use to lay linnen".

To Edward Goodman a silver spoon.

Residue of his leases, chattels, debts, to Joan Goodman and Katherine Goodman, "whole executors", equally divided between them.

Overseers: Thomas Grafton, Humphrey Brian and David Williams, to have 3s 4d each.

Debts owing to testator:
Edward Baker, due at Michaelmas last: 30s.
Thomas Byse: 6s.
Thomas Bennet: 6s.
William Atkyns: 5s.
George Peterson and his daughter: 3s 4d.
John Tege for a bedstead: 6s 8d.
John Tege for 3 ashen posts: 19d.
John Tege for a pair of "bedsides": 10d.
and for a pair of "gimmouls for a cobbard" 3d.
John Tege: 6d and 8d.
Thomas Brook: 40s.
Thomas Brooke, by a bond: £10

Debts owing by testator:
To John Tege: 18d "which I gave my word for John Mody out of the money abovesaid, I owe no more to my remembraunce to any man".

93   JULIAN GOSNELL, widow, St. Ewen nuncupative 29 December 1597, admon. granted to Elizabeth Walter 4 April 1598.

Soul to God almighty and body to be laid in Christian burial in church-yard of St John the Baptist.

All goods and chattles to Elizabeth Walter her daughter's daughter "for that it was her husbands minde it should be soe"; said Elizabeth sole executrix.

Witnesses: Mr Morgan Jones, parson of Christchurch, Miles Hobson pewterer with others.

94   HUGH HARVYE, scrivener, St. Peter, 23 November 1596, proved 18 July 1598.

Soul to almighty God, "assuring my selfe that by the onlye merites of the passion of Jhesus Christ his onlye sonne and my saviour I shalbe an inheritour in the Kingdome of heaven", body to the earth, to be buried "against my pewe wherein I am nowe pewed yn". To the parish for his burial 6s 8d.

"I will that at my buryall that therbe a Sermonde made by some learned honest and discrete parson and I will to be geven him for his paines syx shillings and eight pence".

To the poor 20s to be given in bread at the church on the day of his burial.

To his brother Mr. John Codrington his "peternell", with his flask and "towchbox". To Anne Codrington, daughter of John Codrington, a silver spoon. To his brother Christopher Mylles and his wife a silver spoon each.

To his wife Elizabeth Harvy his garden for life, with the right to sell it if "neede shall so constraine her". If not sold, then to go to Anne Codrington and her heirs.

To each of his godchildren 12d. To each of his servants 3s 4d. on condition that "they shalbe gentle and servisable unto my said wife".

Residue to wife Elizabeth, "whole" executrix.

Written with testator's own hand, seal.

Overseers: Mr. Richard Smythe and Mr. Richard Arthur, clerk, to have 10s each.

Witnesses: Richard Arthur, clerk, Richard [?Smythe, *will damaged*], James Clarke.

95 THOMAS HAYWARD, shearman, Bristol, 24 June 39 Eliz. [1597], proved 23 January 1598/9.

Soul into the hands of almighty God and body to be buried where it shall please God to call him to his mercies.

His now dwelling house to his two brothers Christopher Hayward and Edmond Hayward to be converted into their use equally between them for the term of their lives "my said brother" paying £20 at the feast of All Saints next, which is yet behind and unpaid for the purchase thereof, also maintaining his "now" wife Joan Hayward with sufficient maintenance for a woman of her degree or else paying her £5 p.a. for life, at her choice. To have and to hold the said house to his said brothers during their lives and to the longest liver of them and to the heirs male of the longest liver of them. For want of heirs male of the said brothers, he gives said house to brother William Hayward and his heirs for ever.

To brother Edmond, testator's shop in St. Thomas parish and the lease thereof and all tools and goods whatsoever therein being and the lease of his garden after his wife, who is to hold it for life at rent of 4d p.a. Wife Joan to have the occupying of all his other goods for life and afterwards to remain equally between Christopher and Edmond, whom he makes his executors.

Overseers: kinsman William Weale, baker and Henry Jones, tailor, to whom 5s each for their pains.

Witness: Thomas Newton, clerk

96 JOHN HOPE, vintner, Bristol, 28 February 1597/8, proved PCC 13 March 1597/8, exhibited 28 March 1598.

Soul into the hands of God his creator, to Jesus Christ his redeemer and to the holy ghost "the preserver of me and all the faithfull". Body to the earth, to "remaine untill the day of the resurrection of all flesh".

To daughter Alice £100 at her marriage, the use of the £100 to remain for her maintenance until her marriage.

To the child his wife now expecting, £100, if a daughter then to be paid in same manner as to his daughter Alice, if a son, to be paid after his apprenticeship, "in the meane time the use thereof for his mantenance". If his wife bear 2 children, bequest to be divided between them and paid as above.

If any of his children die before marriage or apprenticeship, their portion to be divided equally between his wife and surviving children. If all his children die, his wife to have the £200, except £40, of which £20 to his brother Thomas and £20 to brother Nicholas, to be paid within 3 days of the decease of all his children.

To brother Thomas £20 to be paid at 21 years. To brother Nicholas 40s to be paid to his master at the beginning of his apprenticeship "to some occupation", and to have "so much as shall double aparrell him competently". Also £20 to be paid at the end of his apprenticeship.

To wife's brother Edward Phelpes £10. To cousin Francis Arundel a black gelding worth £5. To Francis' [?son, *will damaged*], Thomas, £5, to be paid at [?14] years. To his servant Thomas We —— 20 nobles besides his wages. To William Robinson vicar of St. Nicholas 40s. To Mr Arthur, parson of St. Mary le Port 10s. To the clerk of St. Mary le Port 5s. and to poor of parish 5s.

Residue to wife Alice, executrix.

Overseers: Francis Arundle, Mr. John Boulton of Bristol, merchant, testator's brother-in-law William Phelpes and Giles Goughe of Bristol, grocer, "unto which fower I give fower morninge cloakes".

Witness: William Robinson, vicar of St. Nicholas.

97 WILLIAM JACY, clerk, St. Michael, 4 June 1597, proved 26 May 1598.

Parson of the rectory of St. Michael's; sick and weak of body. Commends soul to almighty God "hoping to be saved through the death and passion of my saviour Jhesus Christe". Body to be buried in the chancel of St. Michael's.

To Richard and Francis, "sonnes unto Mr. John Moore all my books and my lute". To testator's brother Edward his doublet and "payned hosse", a pair of stockings and one old shirt and a pair of shoes. To testator's sister and to his cousin, his great chest to be delivered within one month after his decease.

Residue to —— his wife whom he makes sole executrix.

"By me William Jacey, parson of St. Mychael's". David Williams, clerk.

Witnesses: Richard Byllyng, Eleanor Pyllyng [?Byllyng] Jane Bany, Joan Tomas.

98   JOHN LEY, St. John the Baptist, 5 September 1598, nuncupative, proved 4 November, 1598.

Testator "lieng sicke by the visitacion of Allmightie God . . . saide that That which he had was gotten betwene his wiff Joane and him and that the cheldren which he had was hers as well as his and what debts were owen she knewe better than he and therfore he did give her all which he an she had and willed her to paie all his debts and use her discrecion therin".
Wife Joan sole executrix.

Witnesses: Thomas Phelpes, clerk of the parish, Katherine Lewys, Jane Kellock, Dorothy Davis and others.

99   MAURICE LONG, Bristol, 1598, proved 29 April 1598.

To be saved by the death and passion of Christ Jesus.
    To daughter Mary, £23 to be —— son of John upon the day of St. James the apostle next, to the use of the said Ma—— Thomas "my sonne" £20 "on Whitsun —— Agrove to thuse of my sonne till he come to thadge of xxj th yeares. Item I geve ——". To daughter Margaret £20 —— "my sonne John upon thassencion daye in the yeare of our lord God 160—— She com' to adge"; if she die or marry without the —— John then the said money to remain to John, Thomas and Mary. To son John £10, also one standing bedstead a p—— being in the chamber and all the wainscot cupboards and forms and one "payse" and a malt mill and all the cupboards being in the —— bedstead and a standing rack in the kitchen loft.
    "Item I gave —— and a saltinge trowe with the cover and the tallett over the shippinge and all —— windowes within the house". Wife Joan to have the use of all these —— stacks as long as she lives or keep herself unmarried. To —— 2 yokes and 2 strings "my best sullowe and best ayethe to be delivered at my wyfes —— her daye of marredge. Item I geve him my corne wayne to be delyvered within iij yeare —— deathe" also 2 long bows and arrows and a crossbow. The said —— delivered him at the feast of St. Michael the Archangel next; if said John —— or Margaret die before they come to age that then their money to remain from one —— by equal portions.
    To son Edward £10 at age 18. To daughter Anne £10 at age 18. To daughter Jane £5 at age 18. To —— daughter Joan £5 at age 18. Son John to be bound to testator's —— [to] maintain Mary sufficiently with the interest and said son John to be bound to overseers [for] payment of Margaret's money at age of 21 or day of [marriage].
    Residue, debts paid and funeral discharged, to wife Joan, whom he makes full and whole executrix.

Overseers: John Orchard, John Fill, Richard Agrove, Thomas Eerle, Maurice (Mawris) Waall.

Witnesses: John Orchard, Thomas Eerle

"John Smith the Butcher owethe me v li. for certaynes bease and sheepe"

100   RICHARD MANNINGE, pewterer, Barton Hundred, 3 February 1598/9, proved 9 March 1598/9.

Soul to almighty God, body to be buried in St. Philip's churchyard.
    To poor of St. Philip's 2s.
    Residue to wife Anne, executrix.

Witnesses: Mr. Thomas Colman, vicar of St. Philip's, Mr. Thomas Baynard of St. Philip's, with others.

101   WILLIAM SAUNDERS, sailor, St. Stephen, 23 January 1597/8, proved 1 April 1598.

Soul into the hands of Almighty God, "of whome I do not doubte, but that hee of his manifolde and greate mercies, will forgive me mye sinns, And make mye soule to bee perpetuall Inheritour, with hime of the everlastinge Joyes yn heavin". Body to be buried in St. Stephen's churchyard "As nye mye Childerine as mayebee".
    To his wife his house for life, after her death to John Saunders, son of his brother John Saunders.
    His brother John Saunders or "the heier of the houce after the deathe of my wyfe", to pay 4 marks to churchwardens of St. Stephen towards repair of church. His house to remain to the heirs and name of Saunders for ever.
    To Mr. Thomas Tyzon the parson 2s 6d.
    Residue to wife, sole executrix, to receive and pay all debts, "And to see mye honestlie buried".

Witnesses: Lewis Runway, Peter Follen, Philip Evan.

102   THOMAS SETTLE, turner, St. Stephen, "the laste day of Maye" 1597, proved 1598.

"perfecte in mind and memorye". Soul to almighty God, body to be buried in St. Stephen's church.
    To son John all the parcels of goods already given to him, listed at end of will.

Residue to wife Margaret, sole executrix. All former wills revoked.

Witnesses: William Atkins, George Weste, George Hammons, John Hains, notary public.

Parcels given to son John, Monday 5 January 1596/7:
2 pairs of canvas sheets
one pair of calico sheets and a calico pillow-bere
6 table napkins with 2 table cloths
2 hand towels
one down pillow
one carpet for a side table
2 spanish cushions
one coverlet with a blanket "for a bedd"
2 pewter platters, 2 pottingers, one saucer
one "pottell pott of pewter", one pewter goblet
3 pewter flowerpots
2 brass crocks,
one great brass kettle
one skillet, one brass candlestick
one brass chafing dish, one "brasen morter with his pestell"
one great stool, one little stool, one stone cruse covered with silver
one gold ring

Witnesses: Nicholas Woolfe, William Tyler, Thomas Tyzon, parson of St. Stephen's.

103 RICHARD SMITH, shearman, Temple, 1598, proved 19 May 1598.

Soul into the hands of God, body to be buried in Temple churchyard, "there to remaine tyll the lorde —— the Last Daye raise it upp againe to the gloarious Resurrection".

To Temple church 20s for use of church and pipe of Temple parish. Richard Martin, vicar, to see the money "well —— bestowed".

To poor of Temple parish 13s 4d to be distributed the day of his funeral. To Richard Martin, vicar, 20s to be paid when testator's debts are collected. To preacher at his funeral 6s 8d.

To cousin Richard S——, shearman, the lease of his house, provided his wife Eleanor have it for life. To William, son of his —— Richard Smith, 20s to be paid when testator's debts are collected.

To brother David Cecill —— to be paid as before. To [Richard] Reade 5s to be paid as before. To —— Nashe, glover in Redcliffe Street, his second best gown and other clothes. To Margery, daughter of John —— 10s to be paid as before. To Joan S —— his kinswoman living in the country, 10s to be paid as before.

Residue to wife Eleanor, "whole" executrix.

Overseers: Richard Martine, vicar of Temple, [David] Cecill and Richard Reade.

All former wills revoked.

Witnesses: David Cecill, Richard Smith, Richard Reade.

[*Will torn at the top and sides.*]

104 WILLIAM WOODNEY, [St. James], 9 February 1598/9 proved 8 March 1598/9.

Testator "being of perfect health".
   To poor of St. James £3.
   To servant Anne Poole 40s or a cow. To Thomas Packer a signet ring, and to Thomas' son Ralph "my best parrell".
   Residue to wife, full executrix.

Overseers: Thomas Packer, John Sharpe, they to have 10s "to drinke".

Witnesses: John Sharpe, Richard Woodson.

105 MARGERY WRIGHT, widow, St. Thomas, 26 January 1597/8, proved 14 March 1597/8, will exhibited with letters of administration annexed, Prerogative Court of Canterbury, 4 November 1598, granted to Ralph Wright. Inventory valued at £26 6s 7d.

Soul into the hands of almighty God, body to be laid in christian burial.
   To son William Wright of London the fee simple of her old house in Wantage which Matthew Winboult now holds. If William pay to Thomas Wright his brother £20 within 4 years, then William to have the lease of the house "with the rente therein reserved or els to remaine to my executors".
   To son John Wright the fee simple of her new house in Wantage. To Mary Wright, daughter of her eldest son Robert Wright "the lease of the Mores all the yeres that remaine more unto her", a flock bed, a little featherbed, 2 pairs of sheets, 2 bolsters, 2 pillows, a coverlet, a "cafferen".
   To son Richard Wright the lease of the lodge, garden and orchard "I now dwell in, in respecte of the debte I owe him".
   To William Crasles' [*sic*] children, equally divided, all the implements in her new house in Wantage.
   To son William Wright "of Marshfield", a flock bed, a bolster, 2 pillows, 2 pairs of coarse sheets, a new piece of linen cloth of 5 yards, a coverlet, a blanket, one of her "worse" candlesticks, 2 platters, a great pan and a quart pot.
   To son Ralph Wright her best featherbed and best coverlet. To Constance, wife of son Richard Wright, "all my hurds". To Mary Wright, daughter of Robert Wright, a fine sheet, a great brass pot, 2 chargers, a candlestick, a pottinger. To Margery Wright, wife of Richard Redwood, 2 chargers, 2 platters, a chafing dish, a featherbed, a coverlet, a pair of sheets and a blanket.

To Margery Martin a cupboard in the kitchen and a spruce chest. To testator's sister Aldworth of London her gold ring. To daughter Elizabeth Wright of London a piece of gold of 6 shillings.

To daughter Mary Martin her best gown, a great kettle, 2 partlets and a sheet. To Margery Craste [*sic*] a great brass pan, 2 platters and a sheet.

Executor: her kinsman Mr. Robert Aldworth.

Witnesses: Mr. Thomas Aldworth, alderman; John Aldworth; Mr. Thomas Callowhill; Ralph Wright.

106   ALICE APPRICE, widow, St. Philip, 3 February 1598/9, proved 1599.

Soul to almighty God, "my maker creator and redemer through whose greate merite and bloodshedding I steedfastlie beleeve the same wilbe saved". Body to be buried in St. Philip's churchyard, near husband John's grave.

To John Winscombe of Barton Regis, yeoman, 10s and to Mary his wife a gold ring. To cousin John Apprice half a crown in gold. To son John Colman and Anne his wife 10s each. To son-in-law John Ashurst and Susanna his wife 12d each.

To Arthur Lansdon of Winterbourne, yeoman, 10s and to Jane his wife her best hat. To Elizabeth Mountaine of Winterbourne, widow, her second gown. To Alice Payton of Wraxall, widow, 20s. To Susan Payton her god daughter, her best gown. To Richard Mountain, son of Elizabeth, 10s. To John Beake 20s. To Nicholas, son of John Colman, 20s and to Agnes his sister 10s.

To Elizabeth Mountaine her god daughter 3s 4d. To William Aishurst, son of John Ashurst, £5, a standing bedstead, a flockbed, a feather bolster, a pair of "dowlis" sheets, a coverlet, a great chest, a cupboard, a chair, a brass pan, a carpet, 6 cushions, a great candlestick.

To John, son of John Ashurst, £5, a feather bolster, a pair of dowlis sheets, a brass pan, a skillet, a chafing dish, a cupboard, "Rikestack" at Arthur Lannsdon's, a canvas tablecloth, a table board, a coffer, a yearling beast.

To Arthur, son of John Ashurst, £5, a heifer, a feather bolster, a gridiron, a "broch", a pair of dowlis sheets, 6 table napkins and a tablecloth, a brass pan, a brass mortar, a skillet, a round table board, a coffer.

To Thomas, son of John Ashurst, £5, a pair of canvas sheets and a brass pan. To Joan, daughter of John Ashurst, £10, a calf, a brass pan, a crock, a feather bolster, a pair of dowlis sheets, a rug coverlet, a coffer, a candlestick.

To Alice, daughter of John Ashurst, £10, a black cow, a feather bed, a feather bolster, a pair of blankets, a pair of flaxen sheets, a new coverlet, a crock, a cauldron, a dripping pan, a great chest, a candlestick.

All legacies to the 5 children of John Ashurst to be delivered at 21 years or marriage, whichever is first, until then to be "ymploied ymediatlie after my deceas to their and everie of their best profitt". If any of the children die before receiving their legacy, it to be divided among the survivors. If all children die legacies to go to any other children which Susanna Ashurst may have, any gift mentioned beforehand to the contrary notwithstanding.

"Yf my daughter Suzanna her want happen to be suche", overseers to allow her 40s per year from profits of the legacies to her children during their minority.

To poor of Lawford's Gate Almshouses 4d each. 10s "be bestowed ymediatlie after my deceas to make my neighbors drinke". 10s in bread to be given to poor attending the burial.

Residue to William Ashurst, sole executor.

Overseers: John Winscombe, Thomas Ashlin of Barton Regis, Thomas Clement of Bristol, soapmaker, John Reade of Bitton, yeoman, Arthur Landson, and William Tey of Winterbourne.

Witnesses: Thomas Hatton, William Haines of Barton Regis, Richard Cabbe "the writter".

Thomas Dowdin of Winterbourne owes 16s of which 6s to be given to Elizabeth Montaine, and 10s to Richard Montaine.

"Postscript I the above named Alice Apprice doe most earnestlie request Roger Brier to be good unto my sone in law John Ashurst his Children".

107   ELIZABETH BANTONN, widow, St. Thomas, 11 June 1599, proved 29 October 1599.

Soul to almighty God, body to the earth.

To son James Bantonn a feather bed, a bolster, a pair of sheets, a coverlet, a blanket, a pillow, the pillow case being calico, "which bed lies in the little newe Chamber over the entreye".

To son [in law, *deleted*], Thomas Phillips, 20s. To daughter Elizabeth Hellier her best petticoat, her best gown, best smock and best woollen smock, her 2 best cross kerchiefs, best apron, best hat and 2 best partlets.

To daughter's son Charles Hellier a feather bed "in the fore Camber", a coverlet of arras, a bolster, a pillow, a pair of sheets, a pillow-bere of calico, a blanket.

To servant Alses, together with her wages "now at midsommer", 20s., "unto the said Alses Bed" a pair of "harden" sheets, a "black Rug coverlet", and a bolster "to her owne Bed".

To apprentice Richard Peek her feather bed "wherein now I lie" in the middle chamber, a bolster, a pair of flaxen sheets "and the fellowe of the coverlet that my son James is to have", a pillow and pillow-bere, and 20s.

To son James Bantonn 20s which Toby Sheale owes her.

To a preacher, to make a funeral sermon at her burial, 6s 8d. To James Listin, vicar of St. Thomas, 3s 4d. To the poor of St. Thomas 3s 4d in bread.

To Bridget Hellier her granddaughter a pair of flaxen sheets, "which her mother knows".

Residue to son David Banton and daughter Elizabeth Hellier, joint executors.

Overseers: Her brother Gregory Pash, Sampson Edwardes.

Witnesses: Roger Browne, Richard Peeke, James Listin with others.

Debts owed by testatrix:
To Sampson Edwards of Temple, baker, £13
To widow Boldwin, £18
To Thomas Wiles' wife, brewer, £10, to be paid in instalments of 20s every St. James tide, "untill the tenn poundes bee fullie paide".
[To Mr. Lavington upon a bond, £2, *deleted*].
"I have paid unto Mr. Lavinge the some of £14 upon a bond of Robert Stones dettes".
To Roger Harrington of Temple, brewer, for 6 dozen of ale, £1 4s.
To Richard Griesh of the Bridge, 4s 8d.
Clement Pincke 20s "which some I doe absolutelie forgeeve him upon condicion that he deliver unto my Executor, Jonas nessons wives Ringe".
To her servant Bess Cutler three quarter's wages at midsummer next, 9s "whereof shee hath received in parte of paiment, a smock coste 2s 6d, item more a partlet price 2s, so there remaines the some of 4s 6d."

Debts owed to testatrix:
By Mr. Fox 56s.
By Toby Sheale £1
"Item delivered unto Thomas Terlie the sume of £3 12s. for vj dossen of Bullock Bellies, at xijs. the dossen, whereof I have received the number of Nine".
By William Morgan 5s.
By Goodwife Nesson 5s 3d "upon a Ring which Clement Pinck hath".
By her tenant [?Hollom] the tailor, for rent at midsummer next, 10s.
"Item upon a skoare the some of 12s 10d."

108   TOBY BELCHER, merchant, St. Peter, 25 August 1599, proved 16 October, 1599.

Soul into the hands of God "my creator in sure and certayne hope of resurrection to life through Xhst my redeemer", body to be buried in St. Peter's church.

To poor of St. Peter's 5s. To the prisoners of Newgate 2s. To his mother Joan Harris 20s to be paid at 5s a quarter.

To brother Walter Belcher his best suit of apparel, and to Walter's children 20s to be equally divided among them.

To Thomas Keynes 6s 8d. To Lewis Williams a pair of breeches "of violet in grayne". To his aunt Edith Tapp 5s. To Joan Smith daughter of Mr. Richard Smith a silver spoon.

To brother Jonas Davies his green cloak with bow buttons and his dagger. To brother Samuel Davies a gold ring worth 10s.
   Residue to wife Joan, executrix.

Overseers: Mr. Richard Smith, and testator's brother-in-law Mr. Samuel Davies.

Witnesses: Richard Smyth, Samuel Davies.

109   WILLIAM BUTLER, tailor, St. Philip and Jacob, 19 April 1599, nuncupative, administration with will annexed granted to widow 5 May 1599. [*note of grant of probate deleted*].

To daughter Margaret Butler a great press of wainscot, a great brass crock, a brass kettle containing 12 gallons, a feather bed, a feather bolster, a pillow, a pair of blankets and a coverlet.
   Residue to wife Anne.

Witnesses: William Bishoppe, William Moore, tucker.

110   ALICE CHAMBERS, singlewoman, Christchurch, 26 March 1599, proved 25 April 1599.

Soul to almighty God, body to Christian burial.
   All her goods to uncle William Chambers, "full and whole executor".

Witnesses: Morgan Jones "the writer hereof", Wiliam Woodwarde with others.

111   JOHN COOCKE, [weaver], St. Mary Redcliffe, 7 May 1599, proved 7 September, 1599.

Soul to almighty, God, body to the earth.
   To the poor 12d. To Reginald Newes a narrow loom and a flock bed.
   Residue to wife Anne Cooke, sole executrix.

Overseers: Patrick Yonge, Thomas Byshoppe, to have 12d each.

"Also I geve unto my Company after my funerall 2s.

Witnesses: Thomas Byshoppe, Thomas Wathen.

Debts owed to testator:
John Wood 5s 4d.
Emmanuel Biggs 4s 6d.
Gilbert Woodward 25s.
Guy Dosell 4s.

112 ROBERT CORYE, husbandman, St. Philip, 25 January 1599/1600, proved February 1599/1600.

Soul to almighty God, body to be buried in St. Philip's churchyard.
    To poor of St. Philip's 3s 4d to be distributed by overseers.
    To son John £20. To son Robert all his plough harness, his cupboard and table board with frame in the parlour.
    To the 2 sons of his brother Thomas, and 3 sons of his brother William, 2 sheep each. To servant John West a sheep. To aunt Ellen Yong a bushel of rye.
    Residue to wife Joan, sole executrix.

Overseers: brother Thomas, brother-in-law John Havord, each to have 2s.

All former wills revoked.

Witnesses: Thomas Colman, vicar of St. Philip's, Mr. Thomas Baynard, John Aisholent, Nicholas Tillye of St. Philip's, with others.

113 MORRIS DURAND, minister and curate of St. Werburgh, 11 August 1599, proved 31 January 1599/1600.

"So well Considering the Frayeltye and uncertainty of manes mortall Liffe in this transitorye worlde, and how every man ought, by god his worde to sett thinges in an Order, whereby peec and Quiettnes may growe and striffe and Contention may be Avoyded; do therfore now Make and declare this my present Testament and Last Will as Followeth, First my Soule I Commit into the handes of Allmightye god my Creator Redemer and Savior most stedfastly Assureing my Sealfe to have my Salvacion and eternall Liffe Onlye through the Inffinyte mercye of Christ Jesus In and by his pretious death and Passion and most glorious Resurrection Also my boodye to be Layde In Christian buriall'.
    To wife Anne all his apparel, bedding and household stuff, implements, "u-leaseles", and £10, to be paid within 6 months of his death, she to pay any debts owed by her, unknown to testator, out of this £10.
    To servant Joan Monye £4. To Nicholas Hill, weaver, 10s.
    20s "For a supper For my poor Neighbores". To poor of St. Werburgh 10s.
    "Whereas I have taken Paines to make two volumes For boockes my will is that they shalbe soulde and mony made of them and given to poore househoulders most Neadinge".

Executors: Robert Aldworth, John Aldworth.

Witnesses: Thomas Wright, William Melyn.

114 AGNES FORD, singlewoman, Christchurch,12 May 1599, proved 16 August 1599, exhibited in Prerogative Court of Canterbury 8 September 1599.

Makes will "as death is to all men certen and the houres thereof uncertaine". Soul to almighty God "trusting to be saved only by the death and passion of Christ Jesus and by no other meanes".

To brother Ralf Ford 10s and her best gown to his wife. She leaves to her sister Jane [*blank*] in Wales the cow and calf "in her custodie and keeping". To her cousin and godmother Cicely Daulie 30s. To her brother Francis Ford 20s.

To the poor of Christchurch parish 5s to be distributed amongst them that have most need. To the poor of Much Wenlocke parish 20s. To sister-in-law Susan Ford her best petticoat. To Francis Stevens 5s. To Ralf Ford's two children 13s 4d to be equally divided among them. Residue to brother Richard Ford, sole executor.

Witnesses: Morgan Jones, Richard Turner and Elizabeth Davis.

Note that sum of inventory was £23 5s 0d
[*the inventory does not survive at Bristol*]

115   RICHARD GLEWE, St. Stephen, nuncupative, 22 August 1599, administration with will annexed granted to widow Alice 24 August 1599.

To wife Alice £20 and the lease of his house on the Key. To John Sharppe her son £5. To Joan Sharpe and Margaret Sharppe all the wool in the wool loft of his house.

To maidservant Anne 40s.

Testator forgave John Browne a debt of about 40s and Harry Ellis of Bristol, sailor, a debt of 25s.

Witnesses: Harry Elis, John Ablle, Maud Barnys, Anne Boswall, Agnes Browne.

116   THOMAS GREGE, 12 October 1599.

To sister Joan a flock-bed "which I do lyapon" and his second coffer. His old jacket with a pair of sleeves to Joan's son, whose first wife's son is to have a new frieze coat, an old pair of hose (hossen) and an old short [coat?]. To Richard Gay his leathern doublet. Residue to wife Margaret.

117   DAVID JONES, St. Nicholas, 23 November 1598, proved 24 April 1599.

Soul to almighty God, "my creator and unto Jesus Christ my redeemer hoping to be saved by the blood of the same Jesus Christ and by his meritts death and passion". Body to be buried in the "crowd" [*crypt*] of St. Nicholas church.

To Jenkyn Thomas of St. Ismaells £4; 40s to be paid next May 1 and 40s the following May 1. To Eleanor Davis 20s to be paid "at the first daie of may come three yeares".

To his brother at Carmarthen all his wearing apparel. To cousin David Jenkyn, clerk of St. Ismaells, 20s to be paid next May 1.

Residue to wife Joan Jones, executrix.

Overseers: Hugh Waters, John Grig.

Witnesses: William Robinson, vicar of St. Nicholas, Hugh Waters.

118   EDITH JONSON, widow, St. James, 18 April 41 Eliz. [1599] proved 28 April 1599.

Sick in body. Soul into the hands of almighty God, maker and redeemer and her body to be laid in the church of St Peter's.

Her late husband Richard Jonson, deceased, had in his lifetime given her son-in-law Barnard Otely £20 marriage money for preferment of her daughter Agnes. Of this sum part is paid and part unpaid; she now gives Barnard £10 to complete the payment.

To Joan Greaves the flock-bed with appurtenances "whereon she useth to lye". To Gillian Murdock a petticoat, "one of my new smockes" and a white waist petticoat. To Margaret Busher her second best petticoat, second best gown and smock. To the poor of St James 3s 4d ready money.

Residue to son William Jonson, sole executor.

Edmund Swipp and John Berret to be overseers "as my trust is in them" and they are to have 12d each for their pains.

Witnesses: Edmund Swipp, John Berret, Barnard Otely and Thomas Newton.

Proved before Morgan Jones, clerk.

119   MARGARET LANGTON, widow, St. Peter, 18 August 1599, proved 13 September, 1599.

Soul into the hands of God, "assuringe my selfe to be saved and to inherite the Joyes prepared for the electe throughe the meritts of Jesus Christe my redeemer". Body to be buried in St. Peter's church, "as neere my husband Leeche as may be".

To her kinswoman and god daughter Alice Browninge the standing bedstead in the cockloft, a feather bed, a bolster and a coverlet. To William Smythe son of Richard Smythe, a gold signet.

To Anne Smythe and Joan Smythe, sisters of William Smythe, a silver spoon each. To Joan Belshere, wife of Toby Belshere, the standing bedstead "in which shee usually lyeth", and her "Frizeadowe gowne".

To poor of St. Peter's 10s. To Margaret Dudgin 10s. To Mr. Parson's wife her little black gown. To Joan Plevie her baize petticoat.

Residue to Joan Leeche, daughter of testatrix's daughter Alice Leeche, sole executrix. If Joan die without issue or husband, lease of testatrix's house and all her goods to be employed for the benefit of the poor of st. Peter's.

To her cousin Browninge, mother of Alice Browninge, her medley gown.

Overseers: Mr. Richard Smythe, Mr. Captain Langton, "desyring them to be as fathers unto my Executor, And to see that shee be rulid for her owne good".

Witnesses: Richard Smythe, Toby Belshere.

120 AGNES (ANNYS) MARTEN, [widow], St. Mary le Port, 10 October 1598, proved 9 June 1599.

Being sick in body "dothe make and ordayne this my present Testament concerning my Laste Will". Soul to God, her maker and redeemer and body to be buried in churchyard of St Mary le Port.

To eldest son Thomas Marten of Gloucester one flock-bed, a flock bolster, 2 feather pillows, a pair of canvas sheets and a red rug coverlet.

Residue to her daughter's daughter Christian Hamsher, sole executrix of this present testament containing her last will.

Overseer: William Harrison one of the churchwardens of the same parish; he is to have oversight of the goods and of the executrix until she is aged 21 before which she is to receive nothing.

Witnesses: Richard Arthur, clerk, Mrs Margery Langton, John Forrest and others.

121 AGNES (ANES) MASONE, widow of Thomas Masone, baker, deceased, 23 December 1599, nuncupative, administration granted 27 December 1599.

"Beinge Willed to make her will she Answered they say I have nothinge then she beinge towd that her husband made her full Executrix and that all was hers to despose at her will sayinge who shall be your Executor she the foresayd Annes Mason straygte way put her hand forth and tooke her Cosen Ann Clovyll by the hand and sayd ann and therewith all held her faste in presentes of Humfry Clovyll Thomas Taylor Rychard Calde and her keeper and Chrytie Cowarde".

The mark of Thomas Mason, baker, found in the margin of the Bristol Burgess Register 1557–1599 [B.R.O. 04359/1].

122   THOMAS MASSON, [St. Stephen], baker, 29 September 1599, proved 20 October 1599.

Sick in body. Soul to almighty God, father and maker and to his only son Jesus Christ, redeemer and saviour, hoping through his precious blood "shedd on the Crosse for me and all man kynd to have everlastinge lyffe in the Worlde to Come". Body to be buried in St Stephen's churchyard, near the grave of his two sisters.

To the poor of this parish of St Stephen's 20s to be distributed at the discretion of the executrix.

To nephew Thomas Taylor all the plate which he redeemed "home" from Mr John Hopkins, merchant, for £26 which he paid for the redeeming of the same, being 3 goblets double gilt weighing 69 ounces, one salt with a cover double gilt weighing 23 ounces and 6 silver spoons with round heads weighing [blank] ounces and one cruet, footed and brimmed (brymed) weighing 7 ounces.

Thomas Taylor has invested £30 of his own in grain of wheat, rye, "poulte", bran and wood and stores in testator's business; if testator's wife and he cannot [?agree] and continue in the house together then wife to repay the sum, provided said Thomas shall be accountable to testator's wife for the same stock and deliver the same up again if they cannot continue or agree.

Residue to wife, sole executrix.

Overseers: loving friends Humphrey Clovell, goldsmith and Sampson Edwardes, baker.

Witnesses: Humphry Clovyll, Sampson Edwardes, William Well, Robert Frier.

123   JAMES NEWTONN, St. Thomas, [tailor, *deleted*] 27 November 1599, proved 12 January 1599/1600.

Soul to almighty God, body to be buried in St. Thomas churchyard.

To son William Newtonn his best gown, best cloak, best doublet and best hose, a pair of fine sheets, his sword and dagger and some of his books.

Residue to wife Joan, "whole Executrix".

Overseers: William Cirtchington "and my Gossop", Richard Wailsh.

124   WILLIAM PACKER, yeoman, St. James, 25 May 1599, probate 16 August 1599, exhibited in PCC 8 September 1599, inventory total £171 19s 7d.

Weak in body; soul to almighty God, maker and redeemer and saviour hoping to be saved by the death and passion of Jesus Christ and by no other means. Body to be buried in the parish church of St James. 20s to the poor of St James to be distributed by discretion of his overseers.

To son-in-law Thomas Greene testator's best gown, best doublet and hose and best hat. To cousin Thomas Floyd his best mourning cloak.

Residue to wife Agnes Packer, sole executrix.

Overseers: loving and trusty friends Thomas Packer his brother, Morgan Jones, William Lane and Thomas Greene; each is to have 12d as a token.

Witnesses: Morgan Jones the writer hereof, Thomas Packer, Thomas Greene.

125 ARTHUR PANTHURE, Christchurch, 11 October 1599, proved 12 November, 1599.

Soul to almighty God, "trustinge to be saved onlye by the merites of his onlye sonne and my saviour Jesus Christ and by no other meanes". Body to the earth.

To sons and daughters John, Arthur, William, Fortune and Margaret 20s each "in a small token in remembraunce of me, and accordinge to my Poore abilitie, the same to be paid to the boyes at one and twentie yeares of age and the maydes at the dayes of their mariadge or at xxi yeares".

Residue to wife Anne, sole executrix.

Overseers: William Fleete, Thomas Langley.

Witnesses: Morgan Jones, William Fleete.

"thus I make an ende in presence of Thomas Langley".

126 JOHN ROTHELL alias ROTHEWELL, brewer [St. James], 28 January 1598/9, proved 5 September 1599.

Soul to almighty God, maker, redeemer and saviour and body to be buried in parish church of St James "hard bie my pewes dore" at discretion of overseers. To poor people of St James 20s to be distributed in bread among them by his overseers.

To brother Nicholas Rothell alias Rothewell 10s. To brother Richard Rothell alias Rothewell 10s. To sister Olive (Olife) Wheler 10s and to her daughter Wilmoth 20s. To the four children which his brother Walter Rothell alias Rothewell has by his two wives ("Whereof one of them is a woman kinde") 20s to be equally divided between them. To the preacher at his burial 6s 8d.

Residue to wife Alice Rothell alias Rothewell whom he constitutes sole executrix.

Overseers: trusty friends Richard George of the city of Bristol gentleman and Thomas Greene of the same, each of whom is to have 10s as a token.

Witness: Thomas Greene.

127 ALICE SIMONS, widow, Christchurch, 5 January 1587/8, nuncupative, proved 8 May 1599.

To Humphrey Ellis and Margaret his wife, her only daughter, all her goods, moveable and unmoveable.

Executors: Humphrey Ellis and his wife.

Witnesses: John Butler, Thomas Minerer, William Chambers with others.

128 JAMES TAYLOR, clothworker, Temple, 14 November 1599, proved 10 January 1599/1600.

Sick in body; makes his testament "Concerninge heerin my last will". His soul to God, maker, redeemer and sanctifier and his body to be buried in the churchyard of Temple, there to remain until the day of general resurrection "When the lorde as my hope is shall make me partaker of life everlastinge". To the poor of the parish 10s to be distributed among them the day of his funeral. To the Master and Company of Clothworkers 10s to make them drink the day of his funeral.

To his daughter Elizabeth Taylor 40s at her day of marriage and two brass crocks to be delivered on that day; if Elizabeth dies before marriage then the 40s and 2 brass crocks are to descend to Joan his youngest daughter.

To said Elizabeth his house and garden within Lawford's (Laffordes) Gate providing his wife Alice can enjoy it for life. If his wife and Elizabeth both die before Elizabeth marries, then the house and garden are to descend to Joan who is also to have 40s and 2 brass crocks the day of her marriage. If Joan dies before marriage then Elizabeth is to have her 40s and 2 brass crocks. To Richard Martine, vicar of Temple, 5s.

Overseers: his brother Thomas Bishoppe and Owen Meredithe to whome 5s apiece. Residue to loving wife Alice, sole executrix.

Revokes former wills.

Witnesses: Owen Meredith and Thomas Bisshop. "Written by me Rich. Martine".

129 DANIEL WHITE, mariner, St. Nicholas, 9 January 1597/8, proved 5 May 1599.

"dwellinge nowe in Ste. Nicholas streete sounde in body and mynde I prayse God for it"

To wife Mary Whyte, full executrix, all his goods, money and debts, "In consideracon that shee shall bringe up my children to their Learninge and to be carefull of their bringinge up In the feare of God".

130   JOAN WHITTE, widow, City of Bristol. 27 May 1599, proved 4 June 1599.

Soul into the hands of almighty God and to his son my only Saviour and redeemer by whom I trust to be saved.

To son-in-law John Gill one feather bed which is in my chamber with the bolster and 2 pillows and 2 pillow-beres and the red coverlet and the bedstead. To his two maid children a coffer "to a pece" and a platter and a pottinger and a saucer. To Robin Gill and to William Gill "my pige to be delivered to his father". To Charity Glasier a bedstead and a platter, a pottinger and a saucer.

To Thomas Stringer all the stained cloths in the parlour, a cupboard with "the bench there a boultes". To daughter Margery 10s in money. To my brother Robert Coke 10s in money. To Joan Coke towards her relief a pottinger and a candlestick (canstike)

Residue to Susan Plover daughter of testatrix's daughter, whom she constitutes sole executrix. [Written] by me: Thomas Callowhill.

Witnesses: Thomas Stringer, Thomas Callowhill the younger, John Gill, [mark] IG.

131   JOHN WINCHOMBE, yeoman, St. Philip, 2 November 1599, proved 1 December, 1599.

Soul to almighty God "the maker, and to Jhesus Christ the redeemer therof". Body to be buried in St. Philip's churchyard by the tombstone at the church door, between the tomb and the church.

To the poor of St. Philip's "dwelling in the Hundreade" a heifer "which I suppose to be with calfe", to be delivered to the 4 overseers of the poor on 1 May next. If the heifer is not in calf then, she is to be delivered on following 1 May with her calf. "when the saied heifre shall waxe old then that my will is, that the Foure overseers . . . maie or shall sell the Kowe and to buy a yong in her steede Laying out of the poore mens Boxe so moche money as will discharde the paymentt for thexchange therof, and so for evermore to contynue for the profyte of the poore people from tyme to tyme without any fraud or guile yearely".

To cousin Arthur Mowntayne 20 marks to be paid on May Day "come twelve monethes after the date herof", if testator's wife do not marry before then. If she marry she is to pay the 20 marks. If he die first then half the bequest to his mother Isabel Mowntayn.

To kinsman Morgan Wynchombe 40s to be paid at the "comying out" of his apprenticeship. If he die first then bequest to be divided equally among his sisters.

To brother Anthony all his apparel, woollen and linen, except his best cloak, and £5, to be paid after his decease at rate of 5s per quarter.

To Margery, daughter of his brother Anthony, one of the heifers he bought of Richard Brown. To brother-in-law John Ayshehurst a piece of home made cloth, 3³/₄ yards. To cousin Richard Brown a bushel of rye. To Isabel Mowntayne 2 bushels of rye and a bushel of malt.

To Thomas Elliott a bushel of rye. To Thomas' daughter Priscilla one "oewe" and one "chilver" lamb. To neighbour William Offley half a bushel of rye. To Maud Richardes and Agnes Poore a bushel of rye each. To Mr. Thomas Packer, Adam Bynyon, Richard Page and John Ayshehurste 12d each "in token of good will to drinke together in wyne at their pleasure".

Residue to wife Mary, sole executrix.

Overseers: Thomas Ayshekene, Richard Bucke, brother-in-law Arthur Lansdon, to have 6s 8d each.

Witnesses: Thomas Colman, vicar of St. Philip's, John Aishehurst of St. Philip's.

132   JOHN ADEANE, soapmaker, [St. Thomas], 28 October 1600, proved PCC 14 November 1600.

Soul to almighty God, body to be buried in St. Thomas churchyard.

To mother Aves Tyler a gold ring worth 20s. To mother-in-law Joan Tomlynson a gold ring worth 20s. To his aunt Alice Weale and cousin Mary Marten a gold ring worth 20s each.

To children of his brother Robert Adeane, Thomas and John, 20s each. To Mary Adeane, Robert's daughter, 40s. To the other children of Robert, Anne Adeane, Katherine Adeane, Robert jun., and Eleanor Adeane, 50s each.

To children of his brother Matthew Adeane, John and Thomas, 40s each. To his brother Thomas Adeane £10. To his sister Margaret Byrkin £5.

To poor of Awre parish 40s to be distributed by direction of his brother Matthew Adeane and John Byrkin. To poor of St. Thomas parish 40s.

To uncles Humphrey and Laurence Tomlynson 40s each. To Ellen Pickerell 20s. To apprentice Samuel Gayge 40s. To godson Josias Cromwell 20s. To the maidservants of his father in law 10s.

Residue to father-in-law Thomas Tomlynson, "full and whole" executor, to dispose of goods "amongst my daughter and his children".

Overseers: "my welbeloved freindes" Robert Adeane, hooper, Thomas Clemente, soapmaker, Robert Cromwell, to have 10s each.

Witnesses: Robert Adeane, Thomas Clement, Robert Crumwell, Thomas Adeane, Thomas Tomlynson.

Note with will: "John Adeane was buried in the parish Church of St. Thomas . . . the 9th day of November 1600. Jane Deane daughter of John Deane was baptized in the parish Church of St. Thomas . . . the 9th of February 1597".

133 EDMOND AUFLITT alias ALFLATT, chandler, St. Thomas, 13 June 42 Eliz. [1600].

Sick in body, makes testament concerning his last will. Soul to God, ——, redeemer and sanctifier and body to be buried in churchyard of St. Thomas near his father, there to remain until the general day of Resurrection " when (as my hope is) I shalbe made partaker of life ever-lastinge." To the poor 20s to be distributed at his funeral.

His furnace to his son Edmond to have and enjoy at age of 21 years; "yf god shall take awaye my son[ne o]ut of this life" before age 21, testator's wife Agnes (Annes) to enjoy the same for life and if she dies, the furnace is to be valued and equally divided amongst the rest of his children then alive. To son Edmond 20 nobles at age 21 or if he dies before, to be divided between the rest of his children.

The sum of £8 to be paid at age 21 years or day of marriage (whichever shall first happen) to eldest daughter Agnes (Annes); the same to daughters Cicely, Margery, and Joan. Portion of any dying before age of 21 or marriage to be divided among the rest of the sisters then living. Agnes (Annes) his wife "shall not be Constrayned by the fathers of the orphanes to putt in securitie for the payment any parte or parcell of any Legacie. . . For I thinke it a charge sufficient for my said wife to bringe them upp and [fy]nde them althinges necesserie duringe their minorities".

Overseers his loving brother Robert Byde and cousin Thomas Fawkett, to whom in token of love, 10s apiece. Residue to wife Agnes (Annes), sole executrix. Revokes former wills.

Witnesses: Richard Mart[in] of Temple, Richard Wodson.

134 THOMAS BEESE, clothworker, Temple, 18 February 1599/1600, proved [?21, *will damaged*] June 1600.

"writen by me Richard Martine vicar there the 18th daye of February Anno Domini 1599 as followeth"

"beinge syke in bodye, but of sound and perfect memorie laude and praise I geve to Almightie god, to make my testatmente Concerninge herin my last will in manner and fourme followinge"

Soul into the hands of almighty God, "my maker, Redemer and sanctifier, and my body to be buryed by my wife in the Churchyarde of Temple as nighe as maye be there to rest tyll the generall daye of Resurrection, when (as I hope) I shall be made partaker of the glorie and life everlastinge".

To poor of Temple parish 10s to be distributed the day of his funeral. To the preacher at his funeral 6s 8d.

To son John Beese his standing bedstead with a tester, "wherin I lye", the best feather bed, a flockbed, the best feather bolster and 2 pairs of sheets. Also a calico sheet "which was his mothers, yt hath a lace throughe the mydle therof". Also an arras covering, his table board in the hall, 3 pewter platters, 3 pottingers and 3 saucers. Also to son John a flaxen table cloth and a brass crock which was his mother's, £4, his best cloak, best doublet and best breeches, his sword and best stockings. John to have bequests at 21 years or on death of his mother Ellen, whichever is first.

To daughter Margaret a bedstead and featherbed which was her mother's, a bolster, and the rug on his bed. Also 4 pewter platters, 3 pewter pottingers, 3 saucers, a table board with a frame "which lyeth in the Cock loft" and 6 joined stools. Also his biggest brass crock and biggest kettle, a calico tablecloth, 2 pairs of sheets, silver tankard and cover, and £4. These bequests to be delivered immediately after his decease to his brother Laurence Willson of the High Street, together with his daughter Margaret, "whome I geve to my said brother to bringe her upp in the feare of God".

To daughter Martha —— a pair of sheets, 3 pewter platters, 3 pottingers, —— his second brass crock, a pan which was her mother's, a table board with a frame "which is above in the loft", a flaxen table cloth, the lease of Bearlane Racke, 40s. "and her mother's childbedd Clothes". These bequests to be delivered with his daughter Martha to her grandmother immediately after his decease.

To daughter Margaret a bill of £5 which William Lighe, son of William Lighe of Chew Stoke, owes, which testator's brother Wilson is to receive by letter of attorney.

If any of his children die before majority their bequests to be divided equally among the survivors.

His brother Laurence Wilson to receive of his wife Ellen "two fyne graye Cottons to make mony of them to paye my daughter Margaret £4 and my daughter Martha fourty shillinges". Wife Ellen to have the rest of the money of the cottons. "Ellen my wife shall single apparell my children with fine cotton or some stuffe ells which shalbe as good or better".

"I do ordaine that the fathers of the orphannes of this Citie of Bristoll shall not intermedle with any Legacies which I have bequeathed to Margaret and Martha my daughters: neither is it my will that any of theire tutors shall be dryven to put any surties for the securitie of the saide legacies".

To Richard Martin, vicar of Temple, 10s. To John Beese his second cloak.

Overseers: cousin Mr. William Barnes and brother Laurence Wilson, to have 6s 8d each.

Residue to wife Ellen, sole executrix.

All former wills revoked.

Witnesses: Richard Martyn, William Barnes, Philip Downinge.

"Item it is my will that yf my brother Laurence Wilson shall not lyke of the Cottons which he shall fynde redy made at my decease that then he must staye seaven weekes or two monethes then next followinge tyll Ellen my wife can make for his lykeinge two fyne graye cottens or ells my said wife Ellen to paye the six poundes in mony".

135 ROBERT BROCKE, bachelor, Temple, 9 May 1600, proved 2 June 1600.

Being sick in body makes his testament "concerninge herin my last will." Soul to God, maker, redeemer and sanctifier; body to be buried in Temple churchyard there to remain "tyll the daye of the glorious Resurrection in which Christ my saviour shall make me partaker of life everlastinge".

To the 3 children of Thomas Chaundeler and to the child of testator's brother John Brock 10s apiece now remaining in Thomas Chandler's hands, to be paid them at age 15, if "either of them" die, that part to remain to the rest then living.

To his brothers John Brock and Jeffery Brock and his sister Agnes (Annes) Chaundler 10s apiece remaining in his aunt Taylor's hands and 16s towards his burial which is likewise in her hands. To the journey (iorny) men to drink 12d "and to them iiij that shall carry me to churche" 12d. To Elizabeth Durnell 97 pairs of handles with the clave now remaining in aunt Taylor's house. His cloak, hat, best breeches and one shirt to his brother John Brock.

One shirt to Thomas Chandler and one shirt to Jeffery, also to Jeffery his best doublet and a piece of kersey; the rest of his apparel to John Brock and also one load of withy wood to John Brock. To John Brock's daughter "my bigger chest and that which is in the chest and my smale tooles I geve to John Brock". His smaller chest to his aunt's daughter Joan.

Overseers: Richard Bayly and Richard Batt to whom 12d apiece, and 12d to the poor people of the Tucker's Hall. Residue to John Brocke, sole executor. Revokes former wills.

Witnesses: Richard Baily, Richard Batt and John Brock. Testator makes mark.

136 THOMAS BUSHE, tanner, Bristol, 29 December 1600, nuncupative, proved 2 March 1600/1.

To sister Mary Bushe 20s.

Residue to wife Margery, executrix.

"being asked by Mr. Thomas Wathen minister what he would geve unto his two Childeren, the said Thomas Bushe answered, they are here Fleshe and blode, and my Father in Lawe must not onlye be a Father to her but also to her two Children".

Witnesses: Mr. Thomas Wathen, Michael Pyckthorne, Matthew Warren "wyth divers others".

137   JOHN BYRDE, shearman, Temple, 24 January 1600/01, proved 21 March 1600/01.

Sick in body, makes his testament containing his last will. Soul to God, his maker, redeemer and sanctifier and his body to be buried in the east part of Temple churchyard "by my wife Katherine" there to rest until raised at the last day when he will be made partaker of the glorious resurrection in the life everlasting. To the poor of this parish 6s 8d to be distributed amongst them the day of his funeral. To Mr Gulliford to preach a sermon at his funeral 6s 8d.

To daughter Mary (Marie) one flock-bed and a standing bedstead, one pair of good sheets and a pair of blankets and one bolster and a pillow and the coverlet "that lyeth on my bedd wherein I lye sick" and one dozen of pewter of all sorts, all to be delivered to her at her day of marriage. To daughter Mary one little brass cross to be delivered to her at her day of marriage. To son Robert 5 pairs of shears and testator's press, one bedstead with the halfhead in the little chamber, one flock-bed, one pair of sheets, one yellow covering to be delivered to him at the age of 21 years. Said son Robert to enjoy and hold the lease of house wherein testator now dwells provided that testator's wife Ursula may enjoy it for life. To said son Robert "two Platters and Pottinge whichcame from my Mother at Dundarrow" to be delivered to him at age 21 and one brass kettle containing threescore gallons to be delivered at age 21.

To son John 5 pairs of sheets, one flock-bed and the bedstead at the stairhead, one chequer rug and one pair of sheets and one white blanket and two pewter platters all to be delivered to him at age 21.

To daughter Jane one trucklebed "that runneth under the bedd where I lye sick and —— and — flockbed and the little flockbed with —— against —— the fair [?] —— of all sorts" to be delivered to her at age of 21 years or at the day of marriage.

Daughters Mary and Jane to have all his wife's childbed clothes after his wife's decease, equally to be divided. If any of his children die before the age 21 then that child's legacy shall be divided equally amongst those remaining alive.

Overseers: father-in-law Robert Hix and David Sessell, to have 4s apiece for their pains. To Richard Martin vicar of Temple 5s. Residue to wife Ursula sole executrix; revokes former wills.

Written by Richard Martin vicar of Temple.

Witnesses: Robert Hixe, Philip Dowtinge. The mark of John Byrde.

proved by Ursula Byrde, relict

138   ANTHONY DITTIE, musician, [St. Thomas], 26 July 1599, proved 1600.

Soul into the hands of almighty God, body to the earth.

All his goods to wife Margaret, "whole" executrix, "shee to use her dis-crercion towardes my sonne John Dittie".

Witness: James Listun, minister of St. Thomas.

139 ROGER HENDLYE, yeoman, City of Bristol [*endorsed* St. James], 6 August 1600, proved 23 August 1600.

Soul to Almighty God "by whome I truste by his precyus deathe that he suffered uppon the Crosse for me and for all mankynd that he will have mercye uppon me and forgeve me all my synns." His body to the church-yard of St. James "lyinge neare unto my sonne that lyeth there before".

His black mare to his son Thomas Henlye; "to Joane my daughter my hogge Pygge". Residue to wife Mary Henly, sole executrix. "In wittnes of Truthe I putte my Fyrme." Mare and pig to be delivered 10 days after his decease.

Witnesses: Walter Chester, John Gyll [mark] JG, John James.

Debts due by Roger Henly:
to William Graye 4s
to Henry Hobson 2s 10d
to Thomas Wattes wife 1s 9d
to Richard Horte 10½ d
to Ellen of the Barton 9d
to Morris Jones wife 4d
to Margery in Lewins Mead 2½ d
to Thomas Davys 2s 4d

Proved by Mary Henley, executrix.

140 THOMAS HYLL, blacksmith, St. Peter, 28 October 1600, proved 20 November 1600.

Soul to almighty God, "my creator and Redemer and in him I truste to be saved and by non other". Body to be buried in St. Peter's church.
   To poor of St. Peter's 10s.
   To eldest daughter Margaret a house and garden, occupied by Robert Currier, to her and her heirs forever.
   To son John "my grate anndfild in the shope he usinge him selfe". To daughter Dorothy £5. To sons Richard and Thomas £4 each. To son William and daughter Joan £5 each. All these bequests to be paid at mar-riage or 21 years. If any die before this then "his or her parte to Remaine to the Reste".
   To sister Mary 10s.
   Residue "of all my goodes catelles and Tenementes Royall and person-abell moveabell and unmoveabell" to wife Joan, sole executrix, to pay all debts and legacies.

Overseers: Matthew Davis, Thomas Harte, to have "twell pence" each.

Witnesses: Thomas Geringe, Edward Shalle, "Thomas James, parson, the writer heare of" with others.

Debts owed to testator:
John Nottingegame £4 11s.
John Willis £1 7s.
Anthony Wadde £2 9s 4d.
Ryhman the Raker 10s 2d.
William Wade 11s 6d.
Edmond Chewe 10s 4d.
Mr. John Coocke 6s.
John Stones 14s 6d.
John Knight £3 9s 6d.
Richard More £1 10s.

Endorsement: "The last daye of October 1600 was berried Thomas Hill blak smith in the parish of St. Peeters in Bristoll. Pascall Garland parish clark of St. Peeters aforesaid".

141 NICHOLAS MORRICE, sailor, St. Michael, nuncupative 15 October 1600.

Being sick and weak in body, declared his will nuncupatively before his honest neighbours *viz.* Mr Newton being Minister of the said parish.
    One half of his goods to his wife, the other half to his son John Morrice. If his son dies before coming to age then said wife to have all.

Witnesses: Mr Newton, Minister of St Michael's, Walter Fryer of the same parish, tailor, Joan Fryer his wife, Joan Morrice sister of the said Nicholas Morrice, and others.

142 WILLIAM NICHOLAS, tanner, St. Mary Redcliffe, 8 December 1600, proved 16 December 1600.

Soul into the hands of God, "my creator hoping assuredly through the only merites of Jesus Christ my Saviour to be made partaker of liffe everlasting". Body to be buried in church or churchyard of Redcliffe at discretion of executrix.
    To William Wattes a cloth gown. To Agnes Nicholas, daughter of his son Thomas, a pottinger. To Abraham Holder a flask and "towch box". To son Thomas a sword.

Testator's debts to be paid by executrix:
To Hugh Watkins, merchant £3
To Eleanor Bushe 6s 8d.

Residue to wife Joan, "whole and sole executrix".

Debts owed to testator:
John Gravell 20s.
Henry Baker 8s.
Henry Girdler 6s.
Thomas Nicholas his son £3 "which he bowred of me to pay Ralfe Writte".
also 11s "which was in the handes of leg' the shoomaker of Shere-hampton".
also 10s "which he bowred of me to pay rice howell the sadler".
also 8s "which he had of me to pay Richard Lock the Carier".
also 5s 4d "which he had of me to pay William pill of the Bridge for powder".

Overseer: William Whitte, William Howell, William Hasell, to have 12d each "for their paynes taking therein".

Witnesses: William Howell, Henry Appulton, Eleanor Bushe, Eleanor Holder.

143 ROBERT POPE, husbandman, of the Hundred of Barton by Bristol in the county of Gloucs. 24 January 1599/1600 proved 29 March 1600.

Soul to almighty God the maker and redeemer thereof; body to the earth from whence it came to be buried in St. Philip's churchyard.

Best cow to son William to be delivered 3 years after the date hereof. Yearling to son Giles to be delivered to him out of hand after testator's decease. Stoned horse to son Thomas at age 18. Best kettle to daughter Eleanor at the day of her marriage or at age 21, whichever shall first happen. Also to her one flock-bed and one pair of sheets, to be delivered as abovesaid.

To said children above-named "the bettre halfe of my pewter to be delyvered equally among them". To son William "more one Crocke".

Residue to wife Elizabeth (Elsabethe), executrix. Neighbours John Lane and John Campion overseers to whom 12d apiece for their pains.

Witnesses: Thomas Colman, vicar of this parish and Mary Crockett of the same parish with others.

144 CLEMENCE POYNER, widow, All Saints, 2 December 1600, proved 2 January 1600/1601.

Soul to Almighty God, "my creator and redemer through whose great mercie and blood shedding I trust the same wilbee saved, and my body to the earthe from whence it came, to bee laied in christian buriall, in the parishe churche of all Saintes".

To Anne Morgan "my keeper", 40s, a flock bed, "and the bedsteede wherein I nowe doe lie". To Katherine Woolfe the daughter of William Woolfe, clerk, deceased, a flock bed with an Irish rug and a flock bolster.

To Ellen Woolfe a flock bed. "Unto Mathewe Cable his wief my wearing mantle and six lether cusshions". To Anne and Elizabeth Lane, daughters of Edward Lane, deceased, "all other my lynnen, woollen, bedden,
apparells, pewter, brasse, chestes, and household stuffe whatsoever", and
£5 to be divided between them, except the best coverlet and best bed with
appurtenances, to go to John Lane, son of Edward.

To John Lane all debts owed to testatrix, namely, £20 by Matthew
Cable, to be paid a year after her death, and £5 by Thomas Mellen "uppon
a silver salte and a goulde ringe", and all other debts.

John Lane "full and sole" executor.

Witnesses: Matthew Cable, Christopher Woodward, Robert Busher.

145 PATRICK WHITE, gent., Temple 25 March 1600.

Sick of body; bequeaths his soul into the hands of almighty God, his
maker and redeemer "of the merites of Whose deathe and Passion I stedfastlie beleeve to Bee saved". Body to the earth from whence it came to
be laid in some convenient place at discretion of his executrix "Without
any pompe ore extraordinarie Chardge".

The most part of his estate consists of lands and tenements in
Gloucestershire which he has conveyed to his welbeloved father-in-law
Mr. Patrick Young, Mr. Robert Webb and Mr. Edward Bosden on trust to
sell to the person that will give most for the same. Of the proceeds £450 is
to be deposited in very sure and safe hands so that Mrs. Johane Prewett
may be answered and paid £45 p.a. for the interest thereof for life and further his executrix is to pay (out of such advancement as he gives her) £5
p.a. for life to Mrs. Prewett. As soon as conveniently may be, his wife is
to pay £20 which he owes Mrs. Prewett, with interest. After the death of
Mrs. Prewett, £50 of the said £450 is to be paid to her executors, administrators or assigns and the remaining £400 is to be paid to Anthony
Prewett, according to the true intent and meaning of Mr. William
Prewett's will "accordinge to the trust in mee reposed By the said Mr.
Prewett". The trustees are to see good assurance given for the payment of
the £450 and interest.

Of the proceeds of the sale of the lands the trustees are to pay Richard
Ridler £350 "in discharge of my statute ac[k]nowledged unto hime for the
Paimente therof" and they are to take it and deliver it to his executrix. If
they [keep] the money 5 years at interest "as I might have done" those that
keep the money shall give new assurance for the same to Mr. Ridler's
content, so executrix is clearly discharged.

Trustees are to bestow £600 of the proceeds of the sale of the said lands
on a lease of that value to be granted to his welbeloved wife Margaret
White for life with remainder to his daughters Dorothy White and Mary
White jointly for their lives and the longest liver of them. A further £400
coming by the sale of the said lands to be bestowed for buying another

lease of that value to be granted to said Dorothy and Mary for their lives and the life of the longest liver, remainder to his wife Margaret. Desires his wife to do any act requisite for barring her claims of dower and for the better conveyance of the property to the purchaser and to assign the statute of £3,000 acknowledged to testator by Mr. Arthur Placer to the purchaser of the lands "for his Better Securitie".

His wife is to keep and bring up his said children until they be married and she is to have 5 years profits of daughter Mary's moiety of the said lease and 3 years profits of daughter Dorothy's moiety. The children's lease is to be delivered to the Chamber of Bristol for safe custody and the residue of the profits of the said lease during their minority of 18 years or days of marriage (whichever shall first happen) shall be yearly paid into the Chamber to the use of his children, the Mayor and Commonalty of Bristol giving sufficient assurance for repayment to the said children as they accomplish their age of 18 years or marry. Interest is to be paid to the children at 5% p.a. so long as their stock or any part thereof remains in the Chamber.

If his brother Dominic White pays Mr. John Whitson £48 in discharge of a bill wherein testator stands bound as a surety for him and brings or sends £112 or thereabouts which he owes testator, testator's wife is to give him £20 "And whatsoever hee hath gained By the Commodities he had frome me". To father William White £10 within a year of testator's decease if Dominic satisfies his said debt, otherwise this legacy to be void.

His wife is to bestow upon Mrs. Prewett, Mrs. Pitcher, "my Aunt Tomelinsone my Aunt Neale my Sister Hollester my Sister Martin my Sister Anne Younge" a ring of gold each, worth 20s the piece, in token of his remembrance and love. To Mr. Robert Webb for his faithful friendship and diligence to be used in the sale of the said lands and procurement of the said leases, £20. To his servants Robert Sheward and Roger Locke 40s apiece and to servant Mary James 20s; to the boy Nicholas Spirringe 10s.

Residue to wife Margaret White, full and whole executrix.

Declared to be his last will and testament 27 March 1600.

Witnesses: Robert Sheward, Roger Lock, Richard Parcker, Robert Busher.

146 WILLIAM WIDGINS/WIGGINS, St. Peter, 11 December 1600, proved 21 December, 1600, admon. granted to relict Joan.

Soul to almighty God "my creator and Redemer and in him I truste to be saved and by non other". Body to be buried in St. Peter's churchyard "under a greate stonne before the churche Dore".

To godson William James 12d. To god daughter Anne Compton 12d. To John Smithe 1s 4d.

Residue to wife Joan, sole executrix.

Overseers: Thomas James, Humphrey Ellis, to have 12d each.

Witnesses: John Smithe, Thomas James, parson, "the writer heare of with others".

147   SILVESTER WIET/WYETT/WYATT, [*endorsed* St. Stephen],
13 November 1600, proved 29 November 1600.

Soul to almighty God "of whome I doe not doubte but that hee of his
greate mercie and favourabell goodnes will forgive me mye sinns and
make mee a perpetuall Inheritour with him of the Everlastinge Joyes in
heavine". Body to be buried at discretion of friends. All goods and chattels to his wife whome he makes full executrix; residue after payment of
debts to discretion of wife.

"And this I ende upon fridaye being the xiiij daye of November and the
xlij yeare of the Vertuous and gratious Queene Elizabethe" 1600.

Debts Silvester Wyet owed at his death:
[*this heading was added later as debts are all expressed as* "I owe. . . ."]
to John Jones in Fisher lane 40s
to "mye broother Melton" 20s
to neighbour Lewis the turner 28s
"as I suppose" to uncle Andrew Yate
"desieringe him to be goode unto
mye poore Wife and childerine" 50s
to Cromoll at the bridge foot for one
dozen of soap and 2 bushells of salt 7s
to "mye brother Ralfe for makinge
of mye doublet" 3s
to Oteleye the shoemaker for 3 pairs
of children's shoes 3s
to the brewer for a kinderkin of double
beer 4s

Proved by Elizabeth Wyett, relict and executrix.

148   NICHOLAS WOULFE, joiner, St. Stephen, 11 November 1600,
proved 12 December 1600.

Soul to almighty God, "of whome I doe not doubt, but that hee of his
favowrabell goodnes and greate mercie, will forgive mee my sins, and
make my soule a perpetuall Inheritour with hime of the Everlastinge Joyes
in Heavin". Body to be buried at wife's discretion, "where it shall please
hir but not of this parishe".

To daughter Mary, after his wife's death, the lease of his house, with
the single bedstead and "the trockell beadsteade that I lye one, at the
makinge heereof", without bedclothes. To daughter Mary Tristrame, the
press, table board and frame in the same chamber. If Mary do not live in
the house after her mother's death, the "Impellmentes" given to her to
remain in house during term of lease.

To Mary after his wife's death all wainscots with the cupboards in
the parlour and glass in parlour windows; these to remain in house as
above.

If Mary die before his daughter Margaret, then Margaret to have lease and Mary's other bequests after his wife's death. If Margaret die then bequests to Matthew Moore, Margaret's son, and if Matthew die bequests to John Woulfe, son of testator's son William, on same terms as above.

To Margaret, after his wife's death, the best cup covered with silver, "a coopell of the best and greatist candillstickes, the spice morter with his peastell and the bibell".

To Matthew Moore, after his wife's death, the spruce chest, and £4 "which money was £4 5s, but the odd 5s was given unto his Mr William Higgens".

To Matthew Moore the chain and whistle "which was his fathers", and after his wife's death the best flock bed with a pair of sheets, a pair of blankets, a bolster and a coverlet, also a great crock and his best cloak.

To kinsman John Woulfe "halfe a headded beadsteed with a flock bedd and one of the greate crokes, after the deathe of my wiffe if it be leaste".

To poor of St. Stephen's 6s 8d. To the company of joiners 3s 4d "to drinke after mye buriall".

To brother in law David Gothe his best frieze gown, his worsted doublet, his best pair of breeches and his best cap. To Mr. Thomas Tizon 12d.

Residue to wife, full executrix.

No bequests to be given until after his wife's death. "and I will, looke what goodes my wife shall leave after hir death as chattells or ells whatsoever only the guiftes which I have givin in this my will after hir deathe, bee it movabell or unmovabell or whatsoever, I saye and ordanne, that it shalbe equallye parted betwixt my twoo daughters".

Overseers: sons-in-law John Tristrame and Edward Courte.

149 JOHN YEMAN/YEOMAN, grocer, City of Bristol, 5 July 1600.

Being sick of body. Soul to Almighty God; body to be buried in parish church "of our ladye in Recklyefe".

To daughter Katherine Yeman "my best Fetherbed with his bedsteed and with his bowlster & ij pillowes", a blanket, one coarse coverlet, a pair of fine sheets, "my great Pann with two other littell pannes", 2 crocks, 6 platters and 6 pottingers, 6 saucers, 6 pottage dishes, 2 candlesticks, a Dansk chest also a spruce chest.

To daughter Mary a crock and a pan, 2 pottingers, 2 platters, 2 saucers. To his two sons Thomas Yeman and William Yeman his house in the parish of St Mary's in Cardiff, Wales to them and their heirs immediately after his decease; during their minorities his wife Alice Yeman, their mother, to have the profit of the same. To son Thomas Yeman one crock. Residue to wife Alice Yeman and his youngest son William Yeman; they are to be joint executors. Overseers: John Tanner and David Lloid of Cardiff.

Witness: James Bistan [*recte* Listan], Minister of St. Thomas.

[*The will is in a wrapper marked* "my father's Laste wyell & testamentte 1560" *but there is no evidence that the wording necessarily relates to this will.*]

150   MELCHISEDICH ANDROWES, apprentice, St. Thomas, Monday after Feast of St. Paul the Apostle 1600 [27 January 1601], nuncupative, admon. granted 25 July 1601.

"Memorandum that Melchisedich Androwes whilst he lyved servant and Apprentize with Roberte Rogers of the parish of St. Thomas within the citie of Bristoll deceassed being sicke in the howse of the said Roberte Rogers but of verie good memorie; And being asked or demaunded by Mrs Rogers his mistress, what he would give unto her owt of his goodes in recompence of her painestaking with him in his sickines, he then answered her, that he hadd nothing to give unto her, Sayeing unto her, you have no nede of anie thinge that I have, For yow are ritche ynoughe, and said farder I have but tenn poundes in all, And that I have given unto my two sisters that be unmarryed (meaning Susan Androwes and Jane Androwes, and my meaning is that they shall have it betwixt them. The which word[s] he so spake in the presence and hearing of the said Mrs. Rogers and of James Belbin and Ann Hutchin her maideservaunte with others".

151   EDWARD AVERY, collier, St. Philip, 7 December 1600, nuncupative, proved 19 November 1601.

Soul to almighty God, body to be buried in St. Philip's churchyard.
    To daughter Fortune £3 which his brother-in-law Thomas Brewer owes him, one ewe and one lamb.
    Residue to wife Alice, executrix.

Witnesses: Mr. Thomas Baynard, William Maynard, John Avery of St. Philip's.

152   WILLIAM AWSTINE, Redcliffe, —— December 1601, proved —— 1601.

[Soul] to almighty God and body [to be buried] in churchyard of [?Dun——/Dim——]. All moveable and unmoveable [goods] to Catherine Austine and John —— son to be equally divided bet[ween them]. "My welb[eloved]—— shall be my Executrix"
    Ordains welbeloved in Christ Mr Samu—— and John Crumpe to be [overseers] to see his debts recovered and debts that he owes as it shall appear [*deleted* ——s not finished afore it comes].
    Witnesses: Griffin Evan — [and othe]rs.
    By me David —— curate there

[*The right hand side of this will is missing.*]

153   THOMAS BIRKEN, joiner, St. Stephen, 15 March 1601/2, proved
20 March 1601/2.

Soul to God, "my creator to Jesus Christ my redeemer and to the holie
ghost my sanctifyer hoping to bee saved by the meritts death and passion
of the same Jesus Christ and to obteyne everlasting life". Body to the
earth "from whence it came there to remaine untill the resurrection of the
flesh which bodie of myne I hope shall bee then raysed by the vertue of
christs resurrection".

To poor of Awre parish 40s. To poor of St. Stephen's 40s to be distributed by overseers "with what convenient speed they can after my funerall".

To his mother for a token one piece of gold worth 15s, "which now is
in my custodie". To children of his brother John Hamond and wife
Margaret, testator's sister, 20s each to be paid at 21 years.

To Richard and Mathew Birkin, sons of testator's brother John, 20s
each to be paid at 21 years. To godson Thomas Birkin, son of testator's
brother Richard, 3 pieces of gold, each worth 10s.

To each godchild 2s 6d. To the Company of Joiners 5s to be spent after his
funeral. To Elizabeth, daughter of Anne Barnet, widow, for a token, 10s. To
Robert Adeane an oak drawing table. To Thomas Ewen, joiner, 5s. To testator's sister Joan 20s. To brother George his best hat and blue cloak. To
cousin William Vertue all his working tools, to his brother James Vertue 5s.

To Parnell Brewer a piece of gold worth 2s 6d. To cousin Nicholas
Tiler all debts "as is due from him to mee". To cousin William Tiler and
his wife for a token, 10s. To Anne Birkin, wife of his brother Richard, for
a token, 10s in gold.

To apprentice Thomas Read 20s. To brother Richard Birkin his best
cloak. To brother John Birkin his best best doublet and best breeches. To
brother Mathew Birkin the lease of his house "wherein I now dwell with
all the right and interest I have therein", provided Mathew pays to testator's 3 brothers William, James and Anthony 20 nobles.

To brothers William, James and Anthony all his title to a storehouse in Marsh
Street, under a grant from Mr. Richard Stanfast, for which he has paid a fine.

To cousin George Wathen his second best doublet and breeches, and
10s for a token.

Residue to brothers Mathew, William, James and Anthony in equal portions, they to be executors.

Overseers: brothers John and Richard; all former wills revoked.

Witnesses: William Robinson, vicar of St. Nicholas, Robert Adeane,
Richard Birkin, Wiliam Tiler, George Wathen.

154   WILLIAM BURTTE, hooper, St. Stephen, 2 March 1600/01
proved 12 May 1601.

Soul to almighty God "of whome I doo not doubt, but that hee of his
greate mercye, and favourabell goodnes, will forgive mee mye sinnes, &

make mye soule, A perpetuall Inheritor with him of the Everlastinge in heavin".

Body to be buried in the churchyard of St Stephen's. To daughter Lettis his best feather bed with all things belonging, his spruce chest and "the grate ponne of brasse" and the third part of all his linen whatsoever, the standing bedstead "neaxt unto the doore in the chamber where I lye". To both his daughters Elizabeth and Lettis "equallye to be distributed betwixt them bothe, myne Inheritanc that is in the parishe of Newlande". To daughter Elizabeth a flock-bed with all things belonging thereunto.

Residue to "be equallye parted, as the timber and tooles with whatsoever ells, betwixt mye wife and mye sonne." Wife and son joint executors to receive his debts and pay his debts and see his body honestly buried. "This I ende on mondaye beinge the second daye of marche" 1600/01.

Witnesses: John Goninge, William Atkins, joiner, John Pournell, Thomas Tizon, parson there.

155　JOYCE DAIES/DEYOS, widow, St. Thomas, 1 June 1599, proved 20 August 1601.

"beinge nowe whole in bodie and of good and perfect memorie". Soul to "our Heavenlie Father god Almightie, thre personns, and one eternall god, and my hope, and trust is to be saved onlie by the death and passion of Christe Jhesus my saviour". Body to Christian burial.

To son Nicholas Deyos and his heirs 2 tenements and workhouses with furnace and all implements for soapmaking and chandling in Redcliffe Street, one tenement occupied by Widow Tailor, the other by James Wattes. The workhouse and furnace being "in my own tenure". If her son die without issue, remainder to daughters Alice, Anne and Elizabeth and their heirs.

To daughter Joyce Deyos for life, garden and orchard in St. Thomas Street; after her death to testatrix's daughter Anne Dixon for life, then to Thomas Dixon son of Anne, and his heirs.

To daughters Alice Puxton and Anne Dixon £5 each. To daughter Elizabeth £10. All these legacies to be paid out of profits of her property in Bristol.

Son Nicholas Deyos sole executor.

Witnesses: "(delivered to William Deyos to the use of the names above writen)", John Corfield, Thomas Puxton, William Deyos, jun.

"And I Thomas Prin husband of the above named Joyce Deyos in discharge of my conscience, and my Wives intentt, and giftes above expressed, doe consentt, and suffer the same her Will (as much as in my power doth lye) that the same in all thinges be performed, and take effecte, Thomas Prin".

156   THOMAS FLEMYNGE, City of Bristol, 18 January 1601/02, proved 20 March 1601/02.

Soul to saviour Christ "who hath redemed me" and body to be buried in the church of St. Peter in Bristol.

To daughter Joan 20s in money, 2 chargers, one brass crock "that was my father's", one childbed sheet "that was my mothers".

To daughter Agnes (Annes) 20s in money, 2 chargers and "one other Crock that was my father's".

To son Andrew 2 great chargers and "my birdinge peece". To his three other sons William, Thomas and George 3 longbows and his quiver of arrows amongst them. To son William 20s in money, one pair of buff breeches with silver lace, "my seale Skin Jurken"; all things given before to be delivered them at age 21 years.

Residue to wife Ann sole executrix.

Moreover to son Andrew one pair of buff breeches "last made".

Proved by Anne Fleming, executrix.

157   RICHARD HAWLE, innkeeper, St. Thomas, nuncupative, 5 March 1600/1, proved 8 August 1601.

Memorandum that Richard Hawle bequeathed to Richard Boxall of Bristol all his moveable goods and implements in the Pelican, Tucker Street, and in the great hall in St. Thomas Street.

Witness: Mr. James Listunn, minister of St. Thomas, Richard Cox of St. Thomas and Edith his wife with others.

158   JAMES JOHNES, shearman, Temple, 6 September 1601, proved 3 October 1601.

Sick in body. Soul into the hands of almighty God, maker, redeemer and sanctifier and body to be buried in Temple churchyard "before the Clarckes dore" there to rest until the day of resurrection "When God (as my hope is) shall make me partaker of life everlastinge".

To wife Rebecca £15 to be paid within 6 months of his decease; she is to remain in his house "all the tyme of six monethes tyll the said xv li be paiede" then she is to take the house and household stuff and children "upon such rate as myne executour and she shall agree: yf she will not, she is to have her money and so departe".

To his three children Robert, James and Mary Johnes all his goods moveable and unmoveable provided that wife Rebecca shall maintain and keep his said children on her own costs and charges until said £15 be paid her.

Executor his brother David Johnes.

Revokes former wills.

Witnesses: Richard Martine,Vicar of Temple, Thomas Huall, Walter Balton. David Jones of the parish of St Werburg, tailor, Benedict Machin of the parish of All Saints, tailor and Edward Jellis alias Saunders of the parish of Saint Leonard, tailor are bound.

159   DAVID JOHN LLOYDE, miller, St. Peter, 22 March 1600/1, proved 5 December 1601.

"beinge well stricken in olde age and callinge to minde the frayltie of myne estate and the uncerteyntie of my hower of deathe doe therefore in good healthe and perfecte Remembrance make this my laste will and Testament"

Soul to God his creator "in sure and certayne hope of Resurrection to eternall life throughe Christe my Redeemer". Body to be buried in St. Peter's church "harde by my Pewe dore".

On condition that wife Joyce does not claim any dower out of his lands or tenements, she is to have for life occupation of his tenement and garden at the Barres, next to St. James' churchyard, now occupied by Francis Price, also use of a featherbed and bolster, a flockbed and bolster, a pillow, 2 pairs of sheets, 2 pillow-beres, a pair of blankets, 2 coverlets, and as much pewter, brass, linen and woollen as she needs.

Executors to pay her 2s 6d weekly for life, she giving assurance to leave premises in as good condition at her death as she received them, "necessarye use and occupation thereof onlie excepted".

To John and David Jones, sons of testator's son John Jones, deceased, a tenement and garden near the Barres, lately purchased of Thomas Greene, to them and their heirs for ever.

To the poor 26s 8d to be given in bread.

Residue to John and David Jones, executors, "Chardinge [*sic*] and requiringe them and eyther of them as they will answere at the dreadfull daye of Judgment That they agree together as brethren and not Contende about any thinge that shalbe unto them And to see me decentlie broughte to the earthe".

Witnesses: Richard Smyth, George Hardwicke and others.

160   JOHN PITTES, preacher, City of Bristol 19 February 1600/01 proved 11 May 1601.

Weak and sick in body. Soul to almighty God my creator, hoping and verily believing to be saved by the merits, death and passion of his son Christ Jesus "my saviour and redemer"; body to the earth "in suche semely sort as it shall seme good to my executor".

To sons John Pittes and Thomas Pittes £10 apiece; if either deceases this mortal life before he shall accomplish the years sufficient to have and receive his portion then his part so deceasing to remain to the survivor. Testator leaves his sister Mary 5 marks and his servant Margery 20s.

William Winter esquire has by deed granted to William Vawer one of the aldermen of the City of Bristol one messuage with certain lands and tenements belonging, lying in Clapton in Somerset for 99 years if John Pittes (the testator), Alice now his wife and Thomas Tempest (servant to said Mr Vawer and brother to testator's said wife) or any of them shall happen so long to live. This lease is in trust to use of testator, whose will is that Alice shall enjoy the term if she happens so long to live.

If Alice dies before the end of the term the messuage and lands are to remain to testator's son John Pittes for the residue of the 99 years, remainder to Thomas Pittes testator's son if the said Thomas Tempest shall happen so long to live.

Residue to wife executrix who is to have keeping and bringing up of his children and the use of their portions until they shall accomplish the years of discretion to give and govern the same.

Witnesses: servant Robert Redwood, Peter Bisse.

161 HUGH READINGE, gunner, ship "Mary Fortune" of Bristol, 13 October 1600, proved 4 July 1601.

Soul to almighty God, "trustinge through the death of his deare sonne Jhesus Christe to be saved and by none other meanes". Body to Christian burial.

To wife Margaret, all his goods, moveable and unmoveable, she to pay each of his children 20s, the boys at 16 years, girls at 13 years.

Wife Margaret "whole" executrix.

Witnesses: William Dowrage, sailor, Edward Gainsfort, Alexander [?Baymart].

162 JOHN STAPLE, furber (furbrer), City and Diocese of Bristol, 20 August 1601, proved 7 October 1601.

Soul to almighty God and body to be buried in the churchyard of St Ewen's.

To daughter Mary Staple a bed "that Ann my wyfe of her good will doe give some thing belongyng to the bed and bedsteede"; also a little pot and a skillet.

To son Robert Staple "my blewe Cloke to be delivered to him when the yeares of his prenticeship be out yf Ann my wyfe doe not want in the meane while, then I will that she sell it to helpe her selfe and to give him what she shall thinke good therfore or can best spare". Wife Ann Staple sole executrix; she is to bring his body honestly to the ground.

Supervisor: John Grene. Witnesses: William Welles, clerk and Jeremy (Jereme) Skimer

163   DAVID WILLIAMS, joiner, St. Leonard, 6 March 1601/2, nuncupative, proved 11 March 1601/2.

"and exhorted and examined of his christian faith which he stedfastlye acknowledged to the Curat or mynister there . . . declared his last will nuncupativelye as followeth viz I am but a poore man and all the goodes and chattles that I have I give and bequeathe unto Dorothie my wiffe and wold soe doe yf I had ten tymes as muche".

Witnesses: Robert Steward, curate and minister, and others.

164   EDWARD WILSON, sergeant, Christchurch 30 July 1601, proved 7 November 1601.

Makes his will "as death is to all men certayne and the howre thereof uncertayne". Soul to God, maker, redeemer and saviour assuredly believing to be saved by the death and passion of my only lord and saviour Jesus Christ and by no other means. Body to be buried in the churchyard of St. John's in the city as near as maybe to his wife's grave there which is about the tombstone in the middle of the said churchyard.

To Mrs. Anne Butcher a piece of gold of 10s. To Thomas Hynton, fletcher, 20s. To Philip Leane 5s. To Anne Marshe, widow, 6s 8d. To his cousin Joan Kellye his bedstead and bed with all the furniture to the same whereon he now lies. To Jane Rogers, widow, his great pan and 10s in money. To Anne Patche, the wife of Andrew Patche, "my borde with the frame & the fower Joyned stoles that is in my haull".

To Anne Jennynges his best brass crock and best broach. To Anne Patche, the daughter of Andrew Patche, his french bedstead with the flock-bed, bolster and all the furniture to the same "as it is nowe in my haulle"; also his biggest cauldron. To Mary Patche his second cauldron. To Andrew Patche testator's 2 houses and gardens in St. James parish after decease of testator's sister-in-law Joan Wilson; also to her his best gown.

To Anne Hynton her 4 pieces of pewter that are in pawn with testator. To Anne Jones and Mary Jones the daughters of Mr. Morgan Jones, a bowl, a basin, a quart pot and a pint pot. To Richard Jennynges, testator's cousin, 2 joint forms. To John Dee "my pollax and my pooche". To Amy Wauker 20s. To Thomas Marten 10s.

Residue to Mr. Morgan Jones, parson of Christchurch and to Christopher Wauker equally between them; he appoints them executors and revokes former wills. To Joan Marten a pair of andirons.

Mark of Edward Wilson.

Witnesses at the making and writing of this will: Morgan Jones, Christopher Wauker and Thomas Marten.

[Christopher Walker *is mentioned in the probate*]

165 THOMAS ALDWORTH, hooper, Bristol, 27 February 1601/2, proved 25 March 1602.

Soul to God, "my creator to Jesus Christ my redeemer and to the holie ghost my sanctifyer, hoping to bee saved by the meritts death and passion of the same Jesus Christ and throughe his death and passion to obteyne and enioye everlasting life". Body to the earth.

To sister Anne Wryte, cousin Ralph Write and brother-in-law Peter Goughe "to everie one of their three childrens xxs a peece"

To servant Anne £3 6s 8d. To the Hoopers Hall towards the raising of stock for the Company of Hoopers, 6s 8d.

Residue to son Erasmus Aldworth, executor. If Erasmus die before he comes home from sea, then £10 be given to the Almshouse at Lawfords Gate and £10 to William Hawkins on Bristol bridge, residue to children of Ralph Wryte, Anne Wryte and Peter Goughe, equally divided, they to pay testator's legacies and funeral expenses.

Cousin Robert Aldworth executor in trust.

Overseers: John Eaddy, hooper, Ralph Wryte.

Witnesses: Willam Robinson, vicar of St. Nicholas, Ralph Wryte.

166 THOMAS BARWELL, clothworker, Temple, 8 October 1602, proved 20 November 1602.

Being weak and sick in body, makes his testament concerning therein his last will. Soul to God, his maker, redeemer and sanctifier and his body to be buried in the churchyard of Temple near to his wife and children there to remain until God shall raise it up and make him partaker of the glorious resurrection in the life everlasting.

To the poor people of the Tuckers' Hall 4d apiece on the day of his funeral. The following parcels of household stuff are to remain in their several places in his house "continually unremoved" for use of his son Jonas Barwell and his heirs and in default of heirs then to William Barwell testator's son and his heirs, in default to testator's daughter Agnes (Annes) Barwell and her heirs and in default to Margaret Price the daughter of Thomas Price and to her heirs.

First in the backchamber one table board and a frame and 6 new stools, one great chest of wainscot, one standing bed with a tester and settles, one truckle bed and one close stool and the drapery about the board. In testator's own chamber one standing bed with a tester and settles round about and a truckle bed under it of joined work, one joined tableboard and drapery about it and the stained cloths and a cupboard in the drapery. More, in his parlour one table board with a frame and 6 stools and settles about the parlour, one press and 3 cupboards in the drapery. More, in his hall one tableboard and a frame and 4 joined stools.

More, one table board in the backside in the drinking house standing upon two trestles and the drapery round about the board. More, one joined board in the furthest room, also one meal house with shelves about it and a powdering tub. More, in the dark buttery, shelves about it and settles to hold drink. More, in a buttery beyond the same, 2 cupboards, one with turned posts and the other a plain one and shelves about it and a settle to hold drink. More, in his little kitchen next to the same, certain settles and shelves about it. More, in his further kitchen a shelf and a kitchen board. More, in the house beyond the same, certain shelves about it. More, one great stone trough (trowe) in the pavement and other stone trough to hold lye in the backside.

More, 7 boards in the house of Richard Bayly to board testator's hall and 14 boards "more and less" to finish that work in the loft over his further kitchen. More, 2 pieces of timber for wallplattes, one under his neighbour's kitchen bulk and the other under Richard Bailye's bulk. More, 10 glass windows and 20 doors "together with my house wherin I dwell". His wife Joan to have the use of it for life, not diminishing or altering any part. His son Jonas is not to sell or diminish any part of the house or implements.

Testator gives his son Jonas his croft on condition that Jonas shall give to his son Thomas £4 at age 21 or the said croft in as good condition as he received the same. To son William Barwell one green cloak, 3 pairs of canvas sheets, one flock-bed, one bolster, 2 coverlets (one of arras and the other of rug), 2 pewter platters, one charger, 2 pottingers, 2 saucers, 2 brass candlesticks: all these parcels to be delivered to him "as soone as god shall take awaye my life".

His wife Joan is to give to his son William one flock-bed, one bolster and one kettle of the capacity of 4 gallons or thereabouts within a year of testator's decease. To son William, his choice of any of the bedsteads in the forechamber, to be delivered within one month of testator's decease. To daughter Agnes (Annes) the great drapery chest in the forechamber and 3 pairs of canvas sheets, one flock-bed and 2 coverlets (one of arras and one of rug) and a bedstead, one charger of pewter, 2 pewter platters, 2 pottingers, 2 saucers and 2 brass candlesticks of 5s value the pair and one kettle of the capacity of 4 gallons. "Item there lyeth for her in my neighbours the goodwife Matthewes one gowne one featherbeddcase price xxxs and one broach"; these to be delivered "presently" after his decease. Also to her one flock-bed to be delivered within a year.

To Margaret daughter of Thomas Price one flock-bed, 3 pairs of canvas sheets, 2 coverlets (one of arras and the other of rug), 2 pewter platters, one pewter charger, 2 pottingers, 2 saucers, 2 pewter candlesticks, one broach, one brass crock of 3 gallons: all to be delivered immediately after his decease. Also one flock-bed "at that tyme twelvemonthe". To son Jonas 3 pairs of canvas sheets. Testator's wife has 8 pairs of sheets of which he appoints to Jonas Barwell 2 pairs, to William Barwell 2 pairs, to Agnes (Annes) Barwell 2 pairs and to Margaret Price 2 pairs at decease of testator's wife. To Mr. Martine, vicar of Temple, 10s. To son-in-law William Howton testator's new carpet.

Overseers of this will his good neighbours William Chaundler and William Howton to whom 6s 8d apiece. To "my Companie to dryncke the daye of my funerall" 5s. Residue to wife Joan, sole executrix. Revokes former wills. Mark of Thomas Barwell [*a type of merchants's mark*].

Witnesses at the making hereof: marks of William Chaundler (W) and William Howton (WH).

Memorandum at the firming of these presents, that wife Joan is to pay the lord's rent which is 10s a year and 12s a year for the reparations of testator's house.

167   JERVIS BATTIN, cutler, St. Thomas, 7 January 1602/3, proved 15 January 1602/3.

Soul to almighty God, body to be buried in St. Thomas church or churchyard.
   To poor of St. Thomas parish 4d.
   Residue to wife Elizabeth, "whole" executrix.

Witnesses: Anthony Eliott, Andrew Ellett, Edmond Hedges, James Listun, minister of St. Thomas.

168   JOAN BONNER, widow, City of Bristol, nuncupative, 18 June 1602, proved 20 July 1602.

Sick in body. Soul to God and body to the earth. All her goods to her servant Mary Jones her brother's daughter whom she makes whole executrix.

Witnesses: William Robinson, vicar of St. Nicholas, Alice Robertes, Joan Rawlins and others.
"per me Gulielmum Robinson"

169   MARGARET CHAUNDLER, wife of Robert Chaundler, goldsmith, executrix of the will of her husband Patrick White, gent. deceased, 19 October 1601, proved 8 April 1602.

Soul to "Almighty God the Father my Creator, and to his sonne Jesus Christe my onely Redeemer and Saviour and to the Holy Goste my Sanctifier and preserver, three persons and one God, on whome I Stedfastlie doe beleeve desireing god for his mercies sake to forgive me my sinnes, and blott them all out of his Remembraunce, with thanks to him for all his goodnes bestowed on mee. And my body I doe Comend to the Earth from whence yt Came to be Sepulted and Buryed at the discretion of my Exequutor and trustinge to arise at the Laste day, when the Trumpe shall Blowe and then through thy greate mercie to Inherite a place in the Kingdome of Heaven which thou haste prepared for thine Electe from the Begininge.

Husband Robert Chaundler appointed executor of the will of her former husband Patrick White.

Witnesses: George Baldwin, Henry Trippe.

170   JOHN CLARKE, pointmaker, St. James 11 May 39 Eliz. [1597], proved 13 October 1602.

Soul to almighty God and body to be laid in the earth "the mother of all fleshe".

Testator has certain lands laid at mortgage to Thomas Callowhill of Bristol, apothecary, containing 8 tenements; whichever of his sons or daughters is first able to redeem the same for £50 is to have them forever. He also has the lease of a tenement at the back of St. James [St. James's Back] in which he dwells; remainder of years unexpired to be sold by overseers and money divided into 7 even parts to the use of his children Christopher, John the elder, John the younger, Richard, Alice the older, Alice the younger and Margery.

Residue to be divided into 7 even parts, 5 for the benefit of John the younger, Richard, Alice the elder, Alice the younger and Margery; the other two parts equally between Christopher and John the elder whom he makes executors. The other children are also to pay their parts towards the charges of proving this will.

Overseers: his welbeloved friend Mr. Thomas Callohill and Mr. Thomas Packer.

Witnesses: Mr. Thomas Callohill, Thomas Newton and Mr. John Huntt.

171   WILLIAM CROUCHINGTONN, St. Thomas, 20 March 1601/2, proved 27 March 1602.

Soul to almighty God, body to the earth.

To cousin Elizabeth Richmann a stone cruse covered with silver for a token of remembrance. To John Hellier a feather bed, a coverlet, a pair of sheets, a bolster, a pillow. To his brother's daughter Sara Crouchingtonn a flock bed, 2 pairs of sheets and a bolster.

To John King's 6 children 20s each. To poor of St. Thomas Almshouse 6s 8d.

Residue to son-in-law John Bowlton and Ellen Jaine, wife of John Jaine, joint executors.

Witnesses: Thomas Tomlynsonn, John Richmann, James Lystun, minister of St. Thomas.

172 ALICE DAVIES, widow, St. Stephen (late wife of John Davies of the same, hooper), 19 February 1601/2, proved 27 March 1602.

Sick and weak of body, bequeaths soul into the hands of almighty God hoping to have free remission and forgiveness of all her sins and offences by the death and passion of Jesus Christ "who died for my synnes and rose againe for my justificacion". Her body to be buried in the churchyard of St. Stephen's in the city of Bristol near her deceased husband.

To John Webb son of James Webbe of the said parish, cooper, and to John Scamp the son of John Scamp of the same city, sailor, equally between them "all such Coopers Tymber Twigges hoopes and vessells of Tymber wrought & unwrought as I the said Alice have or shall have at the tyme of my deceasse" with all such tools as she has of the hooper's trade and to each of them one ewe or sheep.

To Susan Scampe daughter of John Scampe aforesaid one flock-bed, one bolster, a pair of blankets, a pair of sheets and a rug covering colour red and one chest called the sugar (suger) chest and one ewe or sheep. To James Webbe her son-in-law one shepton coloured cloth gown faced with budge and a silver taster that was her husband's with all her "brokes" and trinkets and one halberd (holberd).

To Henry Davies the son of Thomas Davies deceased 30s and one ewe or sheep. To John Snacknayle son of William Snacknayle of the city of Bristol one ewe or sheep. To Richard Manfeeld son of William Manfeeld of the same city one sheep or ewe. To Henry Tyther and Alice Tither children of Richard Tyther of the same city one sheep or ewe apiece. To Margery Barnsley daughter of Nicholas Barnsley of the same city, vintner, one ewe or sheep.

To her daughter Anne one stone cruse or cup covered and lipped with silver. To "James Vertue my apprentice one cloak of Tawney cloth which was my Late husbandes". To John Lucas son of Henry Lucas of the city of Bristol, hooper, deceased, one pair of hurden sheets.

Residue equally between her two daughters Anne Scampe and Elizabeth Webbe whom she makes executrices.

Overseers "my very frendes" Robert Redwood, John Jones and Nicholas Barnsley.

Witnesses: Robert Redwood, John Jones, Nicholas Barnsley.

173 JOHN GIBSON, cook, 3 October 1602, proved 16 October 1602.

Soul to God "that gave it hoping that he will keepe it safe against the resurrection of all flesh, and I beleeve and hope that I shall bee saved through the meritts death and passion of Jesus Christ". Body to the earth "and then that my soul and bodie shall bee reunited togeather and enioy the kingdome of heaven".

To his wife the estate he has in his dwelling house, to have "during the time granted to mee and my assignes". Half of his goods to his wife, in consideration that she provides for their sons, Thomas jun. and John jun.

Other half of his goods equally divided among his other 4 children, Mary, John sen. Thomas sen. and William.

Testator's interest in house occupied by William Gibbon to daughter Mary.

Wife executrix.

Overseers: neighbours Henry Dawson, William Wawker.

Witnesses: William Robinson, Thomas King, Clement Godell, William Wawker.

174   JOAN GOODDIAR/GOODYER, widow, St. Michael 5 August 1602, proved 20 August 1602.

Sick in body, commends her soul into the hands of almighty God her maker and redeemer and her body to be buried in the churchyard of St. Michael's "as nere as may bee to the place where my husbandes body is allredy leyde".

To Richard Beser, the son of her son-in-law, her best crock and her great kettle, half-a-dozen of pewter, a pair of sheets and one bed. To Tompson Beser, daughter of her daughter, one flock-bed furnished and half-a-dozen of pewter.

Residue after payment of debts and discharge of funerals, to son in-law Robert Beser and her daughter Joan, wife to the said Robert, whom she makes joint executors.

Overseers "my beloved in Christ" Richard Tasker and Edmond Cox to whom 12d apiece for their pains therein to be taken.

Witnesses: Thomas Newton, Richard Billing, Richard Tasker, Edmond Cox and others.

175   JOHN GRAYE, clothier, Temple, attested copy of will, 25 May 1602, proved 13 July, 1602 PCC., exhibited in Bristol Consistory Court 31 July 1602, [*debts outside diocese*].

Soul to God, body to be buried in Temple church "by my pewes side".

To poor of Temple parish 10s to be distributed by overseers within a month of his death.

To son Robert his house occupied by Henry Pantinge, with the lease, racks and garden, provided Rachel his wife have the property for 3 years after his decease, then surrenders it to Robert. If Robert die before 3 years then property to go to daughter Elizabeth, in default of that estate to daughter Mary.

To son Robert £20 to be paid at 24 years, also a pair of good sheets, a good brass crock, 2 pewter platters, 2 pottingers and 2 saucers, to be delivered at 24 years.

To daughter Mary £20 to be paid at 19 years or marriage, whichever is first. If she die then £10 to her mother and £10 to sister Elizabeth. To Mary a little silver drinking bowl and 6 silver spoons, also a pair of good sheets, 2 pewter platters, 2 pottingers and 2 saucers, to be delivered at marriage or 19 years.

To daughter Elizabeth £20 to be paid at 19 years or marriage, also a covered cruse and 4 silver spoons.

Wife Rachel to have for life the use of plate bequeathed to daughters. If Elizabeth die before receiving legacy then £10 to her mother and £10 to sister Mary.

To Elizabeth a good pair of sheets, 2 pewter platters, 2 pottingers and 2 saucers, to be delivered at 19 years or marriage.

To his Company 10s to be paid the day of his funeral. To a preacher 6s 8d to preach at his funeral.

Overseers: testator's brothers Martin and Grummell, to have 20s each.

To Grace Noble 10s. To William Boord his servant 10s. To William Hoell 5s. To Owen Lovell 5s.

Residue to wife Rachel, sole executrix.

All former wills revoked.

Witnesses: Alice Dittye, Cicely Grummell, Grace Noble, Richard Martin "the writer herof".

176 MAUD JONES, widow, St. Peter, nuncupative, 19 February 1602/3, proved 16 March 1602/3.

Her soul to God and her body to be buried in St. Peter's churchyard near her husband. To her daughter Catherine 2 pairs of flaxen sheets and a pair of hurden [sheets], half-a-dozen of napkins, a tablecloth, a pillow-bere (pillowes buer) tasselled, the bed she lay in "with his furniture", the great chest, the table board and 4 stools, a chair, a great platter, a candlestick, a pewter cup, a saltcellar, 2 small saucers and the great crock.

To her daughter Bridget a flock-bed, a half-bedstead and all other things belonging thereto, a pair of flaxen sheets and a pair of hurden [sheets], 3 table napkins, a pillow-bere (pillous bure), a little chest and 20s in money and a kettle.

To her two daughters all her apparel, the best of it to Catherine. To her son John "the shope wholly" and a pair of hurden sheets. To her son Nicholas 7 sheep in the hands of his uncle Howell Jones, a pair of hurden sheets, 2 saucers, a sauce cup (sace cope), a saltcellar and a candlestick. To her "prentis" Robert Yearott his indentures and his master's buff doublet and breeches, a shirt, 2 bands, a pair of hose and shoes and a hat.

Residue to son William, executor, and 20s in money.

Which words she "uttered and spacke" in the presence and hearing of Nicholas Coocke, Thomas James and others.

Admon. with will annexed granted to Nicholas Coocke during minority of executor.

177 MARY KEMBLE, widow, St. Augustine, 3 January 1602/3, proved 11 January 1602/3.

Soul to almighty God, body to be buried near husband William Stibbs in chancel.

To St. Augustine's church 5s to be paid at her burial to churchwardens for repairs. To poor of parish 2s to be distributed in bread at her burial.

To servant Elizabeth Hobbs a flock bed, a little feather bed, a feather bolster, a flock bolster, a rug, a red covering, a blue blanket, a pair of old white blankets, a cotton blanket, a truckle bed, a pair of old sheets, a down pillow, all her wearing clothes, woollen and linen, a great chest in her bedchamber, a little chair "that I was wont to sitt in by the Fyre", a little low joined stool, 2 high joined stools, a cupboard board in her bedchamber, a brass kettle, her second best cupboard, a half cupboard of joined work, a little press of joined work, a pewter pint pot, a "tunne" pewter cup, a brass candlestick, a green curtain of "sayes", a little box and a yellow cushion.

To Joan, wife of Clement Lewis, a great chest in her lower house.

Residue to Robert Watson, sole executor.

Witnesses: Clement Lewis, minister, Thomas Turner.

178 EDITH MASON, widow, St. Nicholas 24 March 1601/2, proved 24 April 1602.

Being sick and weak in body, bequeaths her soul into the hands of almighty God and her body to the earth to be buried in christian burial.

Her best gown to her daughter Suzan and 2 partlets (parletts) and one gorget, 4 kerchiefs (kertches) and one white apron, 2 smocks. To her daughter Joan that gown which is already made for Suzan, 3 smocks, 5 kerchiefs (kerches), 2 partlets (partells), one band and a gorget "& my Stamell wascotte", one black apron and "my best petticote", 2 white aprons and one dyed apron and one coffer at Bristol "& she to give Suzan her Coffer she hath in the country".

To her daughter Joan one flock-bed, one bolster, 2 feather pillows and one coverlet and 3 platters and one pottinger and one saucer (sawer) and one candlestick and one broach and one latten basin and one kettle. To her daughter Suzan one furnace pan, one kettle, 2 platters, one pottinger, one saucer, 2 andirons, one frying pan and one table board, to be delivered at age 18 or day of marriage, whichever shall first happen.

To her son John Mason £4 in money at age 21 if he live so long; if he die before then the same to be equally divided between Suzan and Joan. To her daughter Mary 40s in money at age 18 or day of marriage, whichever shall first happen.

Residue to be equally divided between Suzan and Joan whom she makes executrices.

Overseers: Robert Willes of Freshford and John Shute of Mittford, to whom 12d apiece for their pains.

Witnesses: Thomas Watkyns, James Smyth, John Ipson [? or Jason/ Mason/ Heson]. The mark of Edith Mason.

179   SIMON MAYNE, yeoman, St. Philip, 21 September 1602, proved 16 February 1602/3.

Soul to almighty God, body to be buried in St. Philip's churchyard.

To poor of St. Philip's 2s to be distributed by wife Elizabeth after his death, "where shee shall thinke most needefull and convenient".

To daughter Elizabeth a cow and a "trendle" bedstead in his inner chamber with flockbed, bolster, coverlet and blankets belonging, a pair of sheets and a chest. Also his biggest kettle but one, a frying pan, a spit and 6 pieces of pewter.

To wife Elizabeth a cow and the featherbed next to the stairs in the little chamber, with bedstead, bolster, coverlet and blanket belonging, and a pair of sheets. Also the use of all residue of his household stuff until son Richard is 21, marries, or keeps house. Also to his wife the use of his house with shop and garden for 10 years, paying the lord's rent and other charges, also 4d a year to son Richard at Michaelmas.

To son Richard the lease and assignment of his house, shop and garden, after his wife's decease, overseers to keep it for him at present.

Residue to son Richard, sole executor.

Overseers: Robert Goninge and Richard Ayton of Stapleton, they to have custody of goods and chattels of son Richard, except the household stuff. Overseers to "put and convert my said goodes and chattels unto the most profet that they may" until Richard is 21, marries or keeps house.

If Richard die first then bequest to daughter Elizabeth. If Elizabeth die before marriage then her bequest to Richard.

To each overseer 5s.

Memorandum that testator died in January [1602/3].

Debts due to testator:
Richard Ayton 20s due 25 March, Simon Batten witness.
David Bushe 40s.

William Corye, bailiff, 20s. Mr. Lacy witness.
"Item he oweth me for a gould ring John Neathwaye and Robert Eason being wittnes, 18s."
John Nowne, spurrier, 8s.

180 RICHARD PROSSER/PRORSER, tailor, St. Leonard nuncupative will Sunday 8 August 1602, proved 4 September 1602.

Being somewhat weak in body "beinge Demaunded what was in his mynd to speake it, he aunswered he thanked god there was no yll in his mynde, And then he said all that ever I have I do give unto my Wiffe Katheren if yt weare more. And I do make her my Executrix. And I have no body els for to give yt unto".

Witnesses: Katherine Williams, Anne Powell and others.

Proved by Katherine Prorser, relict and executrix

181 JOHN STONES, weaver, St. Philip, 2 June 1602, nuncupative, proved 12 June 1602.

Soul to almighty God, body to be buried in St. Philip's churchyard.
    To neighbours John Goomley, chandler, and John Cooper, weaver, both of St. Philip's, all his goods, chattels and debts, they to be executors and pay all debts owed.

Witnesses: Thomas Dollyn, yeoman, William Offley, spurrier, Edmond Wallis, weaver, Gillian wife of Thomas Dollyn, all of St. Philip's.

182 MARGARET SYON, widow, St. Peter 13 June 1602, proved 5 August 1602.

Sick in body. Soul to almighty God, creator and redeemer, in whom she trusts to be saved and by none other. Body to be buried in the churchyard of St. Peter's "as neare as is poscibell to my housband etc.".
    All the goods in her shop to her two apprentices viz. Ambrose Dornell and Richard Palmer and she gives them the residue of their years yet to come. To Anne Sommers her holiday gown. To Catherine Hose her petticoat with the red fringe (fronge). To god-daughter Dorothy Hounte one of the biggest (bidgeste) chargers. To the poor of the parish of St. Peter's 2s 6d. To Margery Sommers 2 pottingers and a saucer. To Thomas James "our parson", her husband's doublet.
    Residue to her sister Dorothy Hanine [?], sole executrix.

Overseer: Mr. Edward Bosden and for his painstaking, 12d.

Witnesses: William Hunt and Thomas James, parson and writer hereof, with others.

183 JOHN TYPPETT, lighterman, St. Augustine, 5 April 1602, proved 20 May 1602.

Soul to almighty God, body to be buried in St. Augustine's church.

To repair of church 6s 8d. To daughter Alice Typpett the lease of his house and garden in Frog Lane, occupied by John Cooke.

To sons William, Nicholas, John and Clement 20s each. To Clement the lease of his garden at St. Augustine's Green.

Residue to wife Jane "whom I do very willingly make my Sole executrixe".

Overseers: "my welbeloved neygbours John Birde the elder, and Humffrey Brian".

Witnesses: Clement Lewis, minister, John Birde, sen., Edmond Smythe.

Debts owed to testator:
John Shale of Tewkesbury, 10s for lime.
Elizabeth Pavy, widow, of Clifton, 2s for faggots, 12s and 4s for lime.
Peter Roe of Bridgwater, 53s for coals.
Parishioners of St. Augustine, in his capacity as churchwarden, 14s.

Debts owed by testator:
To Robert Woodruffe for coals: 3s 4d.
To Mr. Reade for coals: 26s.
To Thomas Woodwale: 33s 4d.
To John Birde, sen.: 50s.
To Frances Popam: 16s 6d.
To Mr. William Gibbes: £3
To Mr. William Vawer: £3 18s.
To Anne Browne [?20s, *will blotted*]
To Mr. Andrew Yattes: 15s.
To Richard Clarke, baker: 4s.
To Margaret Bufford: 3s.
To "Mr. Docter" James: 3s 4d.
To the meal man: 10s.
To Alice Typpett: 6s.
To Humfrey Bryan: 12s.
To Anthony Vaughan: 2s 8d.
To goodman Williams 2s 8d.

184 JOHN WALLIS, labourer, Redcliffe, 4 May 1602.

Soul to almighty God and body to the earth. All his goods and chattels to wife Margery, executrix, who is to pay his debts and to give to his godson John Wallis (his brother's son) a bond or obligation under her hand binding herself and her executors to pay him within one month after her decease £8 "of the gwifte of me John Wallis". Revokes former wills.

Witnesses: Thomas Pitt, William Howell.

185   RICHARD WELSHE, tailor, St. Stephen, nuncupative, proved 21 March 1602/3.

"being asked by Wylliam Atkins his neighbour . . . to whome he would give his goodes, if God should call him he the said Richard Welsh answered and said, All that I have, I give unto Elizabeth my wife, and I would to God it were more or better for her. And being farder asked by the said William Atkins, what he would give unto his daughters, he then answered They are all my wives aswell as myne, and therfore I know shee will be carefull of them",

To his 2 elder daughters a ring each worth 10s.

Wife "full and whole Executor, and I give her all that I have. And I do praie her to have a Care unto the bringing upp of my children And to see my two eldest daughters well placed, That they maie do good unto their sisters. All which wordes or speecheis were so spoken and delivered by the said Richard Welshe as he laie sick in his bedd in manner aforesaid in the presence and hearinge of the said Wylliam Atkins and John Gunninge and others".

"A note of such goodes as I Richard Welshe have lyeing abroad".

"Imprimis I lefte in John Stephens handes of St. Ives nyne barrells of salte and seaven empty Casks, and in Wylliam Goldsmithes hande of the same two new hoggesheds, two barrells and monie for a barrell of beere".

Debts owing to testator:
William Baylie of St. Ives 30s.
James Trunhale of the same 5s.
Thomas Hoare of Dungarvan in Ireland 7s 6d.
Gilbert Noble of the same 10s. "which I lent him at Coombe"
Morris Harvie of the same "uppon his bill"10s.
Salisbury of Frome, Som. 18s.
Thomas Baylie in Marsh Street 59s 6d.
John Fynn of the same   6s.
John Masters 36s 8d.
Edmund Dee 8s.
goodman Floyd 7s 6d.
Gabriel Panter 8s.
Thomas Dee £5 6s 8d.

Debts owed by testator:
"there is an Accompt betwixt Mr. Pitcher and me, and I think I rest in his debt about 40s."

186   WILLIAM WHITE, mariner, City of Bristol, 7 March 39 Eliz [1596/7], proved 23 December 1602.

Makes his last will and testament "myndinge and entendinge god willing a voyage into the seas". Commits his body to the earth "wherehence it

Came" hoping to be saved by the precious death and burial of my only saviour and redeemer Jesus Christ and by no other means.

All his goods, chattels and household stuff to wife Joan late wife of Robert Bayneham deceased whom he makes sole executrix. "And thus I make an end".

Witnesses: Thomas Langley (scr') 1596, William Stydman.

APPENDIX

Six wills dated 1559 found among the Records
of the Dean & Chapter of
Bristol Cathedral

187   CICELY LADY BERKELEY, widow of Sir Thomas Berkeley, 1559 [no month].

Soul to almighty God, body to be buried in Cathedral Church of the Holy Trinity of Bristol, near the grave of her husband "in good and decente manner".

Her 3 great silver double gilt bowls with covers and 2 "prise pottes" of silver parcel gilt to be sold by executors and overseers to defray funeral expenses, remembrance services after one month and one year, and "dedes of charytye to the poore". Daughter Frances Daverse to have first right to purchase plate if she wishes.

To Frances' son Maurice Barkley her best standing cup and cover of silver double gilt, a little silver double gilt salt with cover, also £20, part of £77 which her son-in-law Richard Daverse "hath in his handes of myne", a featherbed with a pair of sheets and all other things belonging.

Daughter Frances to give her "derlye belovid frinde and kinsman Sir Nycholas Arnolde knighte" a gold ring called the "Rocke saphier" for a remembrance.

To her daughter's child Eleanor Barkley £37, part of the sum of £77 above, and £3 to make up the total of £40, her second best silver double gilt standing cup and cover, her best gold ring, the feather bed "that I lye upon", a pair of sheets and all other things belonging, with the tester and bedstead, and another featherbed, one of the 2 having the newest coarser ticking.

To her daughter's child Anne Berkley £20, remainder of the sum of £77 above, her second best gold ring, and the other featherbed with the newest coarser ticking.

To Frances Barkley and Cicely Daverse, her daughter's children, a little gold ring each. To son-in-law Richard Daverse a silver beer pot and 10 wethers in the keeping of Humphrey Busshe.

To Mistress Paine a little silver goblet and a pair of fine sheets. To John Fawkner her old servant a silver piece, the featherbed he lies on with a pair of sheets and bedclothes belonging and a black gown.

To servant Humphrey Bushe the bed he lies on, with bolster, a pair of sheets and bedclothes belonging, a white nag, the rest of the wethers in his keeping, a black coat, a brass pot, a pan, a spit and a candlestick.

To servant Thomas Myddleton 40s and a black coat. To servant John Eaton 20s and a black coat. To servant Ledongton 40s to buy a cow, and a black coat. To servant Edith 6s 8d above her wages. To servant Anne a featherbed, a bolster, a coverlet, a pair of blankets, 2 pairs of sheets, 4 platters, 4 pottingers and 4 saucers.

To Mistress Jones a silver gilt spoon, and to her son Hugh, Lady Berkeley's godson, a little silver beer pot. To "mother Siball my olde woman the bedd that she lyeth upon" and all things belonging, 2 pairs of canvas sheets, a mantle, a frieze gown, and some of her smocks "to my daughters discretyon" and 20s.

All napery and linen clothes not otherwise bequeathed to be equally divided between daughter Frances and her daughters.

To Edward Barkley her daughter's eldest son, son and heir to Maurice Barkley esq. deceased, a gold chain and cross "my Flower of Dymondes", a basin and ewer of silver parcel gilt with the Berkeley Arms, 3 silver parcel gilt bowls and covers with the Arms on top, her spice —— of silver double gilt, a stone cup garnished with silver, 6 of her best silver spoons, her best velvet gown, best down featherbed, best coverlet, 2 pairs of fustians, 2 pairs of fine holland sheets of 3 breadths each with the bolsters and down pillows belonging, the tester of crimson velvet and cloth of gold, and bedstead belonging. Also her best tablecloth of fine diaper with the "coberte" cloth towel and fine diaper napkins matching, and "a greate fyne shete comonlye called a chylde bed shete". Also 2 other featherbeds "the beste nexte to my two beste beddes" with all things belonging, "a whole garnysshe of pewter vesshul with the charger", and the great brass pot and the greatest pan.

To daughter Frances Daverse her tablet of gold, her "great bowle bason of silver", the best silver salt, double gilt, 3 silver goblets with cover, her third silver double gilt standing cup and cover, a silver ale pot, a stone pot and cover garnished with silver gilt, 6 of her best silver spoons. Also her second best down featherbed with all things belonging, and all her apparel not otherwise bequeathed. Also "one hole garnisshe of pewter vesshell with the charger", her broad diaper tablecloth with "the towell Cobert clothe", a dozen matching diaper napkins and a pair of fine holland head sheets.

To daughter Frances, and grandson Edward Barkley, the lease and term of years in her mansion house at the Gaunts, Frances having the use for life, remainder to Edward. To Edward a silver gilt spoon. To Frances and Edward 6 silver spoons, next best to those bequeathed before.

Executors: daughter Frances and grandson Edward Barkeley, trusting them "to paye my dettes and to do dedes of charitie for my soule and Christen soules to the pleasure of allmightie god".

Overseers: nephew Arthur Porter esq. and George Jones gent. Arthur to have £10 to be paid "at the daye of twelfemonethes mynde" or before.

Residue to be divided between daughter Frances, Maurice Barkeley, and Frances' daughters.

Witnesses: George Jones, Maurice Barkeley her daughter's son, Richard Williams, Town Clerk of Bristol, William Eydon, schoolmaster of St. Augustine's, her servant Humphrey Busshe and others.

188 DAVID HARTE, burgess, Temple, 13 August 1559.

"Vexed with sicknes in my bodye"

Soul to almighty God, "and to our blessed Ladye Sainte Marye and to all the hollye companye of heavin", body to be buried in Temple churchyard.

To son John Harte a featherbed and a little posnett which his grandmother left him. To son Richard Harte the lease of his house on condition that he pays the rent to proctors of Temple church and carries out repairs. Also he shall not pledge, alienate of sell the house for the term of years left without consent of Mr. John Stone and John Bovye, "and that upon a Reasonable cause of them knowen redowndinge towardes a better comodytye to the same Rychard and his heires". Richard to forfeit his claims under the will if he does not abide by these terms.

Residue to son Richard, executor, "to dispose all thinges therin mencyoned as he shall answer before god and man, and to his helpe and succour I have ordeined Mr. John Stone and John Bovye, oversears".

To Mr. Stone 5s and to John Bovye his best gown and 10s.

To Burnam Evan 40s and a flockbed. To Frances [?Harte] a silver pin "of the least sort", a kerchief and a partlet.

To Thomas Grene his apprentice a pair of good middle shears with all things belonging.

Witnesses: sir John Pyll, vicar of Temple, Mr. John Stone, John Bovye, William Stone with others.

189 WILLIAM HARTE, baker, Christchurch, 1 July 1559.

Soul to almighty God, body to be buried in Christchurch.

To son John Harte and daughters Alice, Elizabeth and Cicely 20s each. If any children "dye before the other then this iiijli to be distributed betwixte them that be alive and so the Longest liver of them to enjoye all".

Residue to wife Katherine, "hole executrix".

Overseer: Thomas Barry, goldsmith.

Witnesses: sir Thomas Pinchin, Thomas Barry, John Parsivall.

190 JOHN MERICKE, 5 May 1559.

Soul to almighty God, body to be buried "emongest christyan people".

To son Thomas his best bed, a flockbed, 4 of his best crocks, 6 candlesticks, 3 platters, 3 pottingers, 3 saucers, his best gown furred with black coney, a gown faced with camlet, a spruce leather coat, a doublet with satin sleeves, a "fryshadow cloke", a worsted cassock and a silver pint cup.

Edmund Grove to have son Thomas to live with him immediately after testator's decease. Testator's wife to deliver all bequests to Thomas over to Edmund Grove at end of 12 months, to Thomas' use. If Thomas die within 12 months all bequests remain to wife, sole executrix.

Overseers: Morgan Melyne and Edmund Grove, to have a crown each.

Witnesses: John Restall, clerk, Morgan Meline, Edmund Grove, Thomas Merith, with others.

191 RICHARD MORSE, St. Philip, 14 August 1559.

Soul to almighty God, body to be buried in St. Philip's church.
To poor of parish 5s in bread.
To daughter Ellen his "pewke" gown. To Harry Jeffreis a velvet "in graine" furred gown. To John Ryder his fox furred gown. To William Benbowe a "browne blewe Jacket garded with velvet".
Residue to wife Haggas, executrix. To his wife his house in Old Market for life, then to daughter Ellen and heirs. To wife the rent of his house which William Benbowe lives in, remainder to daughter Ellen.

Overseers: Henry Jeffreys, John Rydere.

Witnesses: Thomas Colman, William Benbowe "with othermore".

192 RICHARD WHITE, merchant, St. Stephen, 17 July 1559.

Soul to almighty God, body to Christian burial.
To daughter-in-law Anne Stevins all the iron "that I lefte in the towne of Rose in Ireland at my Laste coming therhence". Also a quarter of all his brass and pewter, a featherbed, a feather bolster, a good pair of sheets, a red or yellow coverlet "at her choyse", and the green cloth.
To sister Joan £24 "of newe money of quene Maryes coine currant in England" left in Rose. To daughter Margery his "terse" [?*third*] part of the ship Julian with masts, sails, anchors, cables, hawsers, "tacklinges, Abiliments", ordnance and munitions, and a third of the cargo. To Margery all his salt "which is in my shippe in my house at Bristoll".
£6 owed by James, his brother's son, forgiven, and his second best gown given to James. To brother's son William White of Rose, his best doublet, jacket, and best gown. 2½ stones of iron owed by William forgiven.
To sister-in-law Ellen Pymase, widow, of Rose, for the use of her children, £5 current Irish money, 30s which Ellen owed forgiven.
To building of Rose parish church £5 current Irish money.

To daughter Elizabeth, wife of Thomas Smith, half his plate, and £60 current English money "owt of my golde that I lefte in my coffer in Ireland".

To poor of Bristol £15 to be distributed by overseers. Debt owed by "Ryse the Sherman" forgiven. Debt of £20 owed by Thomas Smithes, son-in-law, forgiven.

To daughter Margery, wife of John Welshe, his house on the Key, to her and her heirs for ever, remainder to daughter Elizabeth Smithes and her heirs, remainder to children of his brother William White.

To William Doninge "the gonne which I bought of hym". To Robert Mursey of Kelkney [?*Kilkenny*] his crossbow and quarrels. To Mr. Archell of Kelkney his russet coat "and I do surrender hym the mead which I had of hym".

To Thomas White his brother's son of Rosse his cut jerkin and camlet (chamblet) doublet. To cousin Ellen Neyle of Bristol 20s. To Thomas White 4 shirts. To the poor £8.

Executor: John Welshe, son-in-law, to whom the residue of goods.

Overseers: Thomas Symons, William Doninge of Bristol, to have 20s each.

Witnesses: Mr Hugh Jones, parson of St. Stephen's, Thomas Simons, merchant, William Doninge, tailor, George Warren, shipwright, and others.

BIOGRAPHICAL NOTES

Sources Consulted

Primary Sources

Burgess register 1590–1598 [BRO 04358]
Burgess register 1557–1599 [BRO 04359/1]
Great Orphan Book and Book of Wills No. 1 1380–1633 [BRO 04421/1]
Book of Wills No. 3 1595–1633 [BRO 04421/3]
Burial registers where they have survived for appropriate parishes.

Printed Sources

Calendar of the Bristol Apprentice Book :
Part I 1532–1542 ed. D. Hollis [BRS vol. XIV 1948]
Part II 1542–1552 ed. E. Ralph and N.M. Hardwick [BRS vol. XXXIII 1980]
Part III 1552–1565 ed. E. Ralph [BRS vol. XLIII 1992]

Bristol Apprentice Book   1566–1573
                              1573–1579
                              1579–1586
Transcribed by Margaret McGregor for Bristol and Avon Family History
    Society.
The Clergy of Bristol, c. 1530–c. 1570, doctoral thesis by Martha Clayton
    Skeeters for University of Texas at Austin [1984].

Notes:

burgess entries include reason for qualification as freeman, *viz.* by apprenticeship, marriage, patrimony or purchase.

burials are in expected parish, unless otherwise stated.

where it is uncertain whether the information found relates to the correct
person /family, the entry is prefaced thus: ?

1.   FECHETT, Richard, 1546
     (also Fletcher)
     ordained deacon 24 Mar. 1520, priest, 22 Sept. 1520 [Bath and
     Wells] to title of Hospital of St. Mark
     brother, St. Mark, 11 Sept. 1534, at dissolution 9 Dec. 1539,
     possibly Oxford, B. Gram. 10 July 1531

3.   DOLE, Elizabeth, 1570
     Thos. Dole, smith and wf. Eliz. take 6 appr. 7 May 1540–10
     Nov. 1547 inc. s. Ralph 15 Apr. 1543

4.   COSTON, Francis, 1571
     Humph. Coston, orchelmaker and wf. Lucy take John Lewelyn
     appr. 30 May 1553
     burg. 18 Aug. 1563, merchant s.o. Humph. Coston, merch.

5.   APOWELL, Edward, 1571
     burg. 11 Oct. 1562, vintner, m. Kath. d. of Walt. Harrolde
     bur. 23 Aug. 1571

7.   STONE, William, 1571
     ? burg. 6 Dec. 1561, beerbrewer, appr. John Stone, brewer

8.   MAY, Harry, 1573
     burg. 3 Dec. 1571, Hen. Maye, mariner, m. Cath. formerly wf.
     Edw. Powell vintner.
     bur. 11 June 1573

9.   BECK, Joan, 1573
     ? John Beck, wiredrawer and wf. Joan take 5 appr. 31 July 1559
     10 Mar. 1569/70
     ? burg. John Becke 2 Aug. 1564 appr. Thos. Tyson merchant.
     bur. 23 May 1573

10. COMPANNE, Jane, als. Fyanne, 1574
     Dennys Fian, brewer and wf. Jane take Adam Lewis, Chepstow,
     appr. 23 Aug. 1554
     bur. 18 Apr. 1574

13. HYLL, Alan, 1574
     Alan Hyll, merchant and wf. Matilda take John Seybryght,
     Blakestone, Worcs. appr. 22 Sept. 1539
     Allen Hill, merchant, appointed by Common Council to office of
     salt meter, *c*. Apr. 1570
     bur. 9 Dec. 1574

14. HOPKYN, William, 1574
     bur. 19 Apr. 1574 "Ahopkyn"

15.   HUNT, George, 1574
       Geo. Hunt, whitawer and wf. Ag. take 5 appr. 3 July 1553–29
       July 1573

16.   LEWIS/LEUES, Agnes, 1574/5
       see Lewis, John

17.   LEWIS, John, 1574
       ? burg. John Lewes, whitawer, 9 Aug. 1563, s.o. Rog. Lewis,
       whitawer
       ? burg. John Lewes, glover, 13 Nov. 1563, appr. Walt. Davies

18.   NEWMAN, Richard, 1574
       bur. 11 Dec. 1574

19.   NORTHALL, Rowland, 1574
       burg. 20 May 1564, pewterer s.o. John Northall.
       Rowl. Northall, pewterer. and wf. Eliz. take Thos. Colton,
       Pitchford, Salop. appr. 1 Mar. 1565/6
       bur. 1 May 1574

20.   TURNER, William, 1574
       burg. 13 Jan. 1570/1, fine 44s 6d.
       Wm. Turner, weaver and wf. Maud take John Trehearne of
       "Skenffrut", appr. 15 Nov. 1571,
       bur. 12 May 1574

21.   WAWEN, Edward, 1574
       burg. 18 June 1563, singingman, m. Joan d.o. Thos. Rawleins,
       weaver

22.   YEMAN, William, 1574
       burg. 10 Dec. 1560, appr. to Arth. Ricarte, glover.
       Wm. Yeman, glover and wf. Joan take 3 appr. 26 July 1561–31
       July 1570

23.   DAVIES, Morgan, 1592
       ? burg. Morgan Davies [no trade] 2 Nov. 1588, unspecified fine
       bur. 19 Feb. 1591/2

24.   ANDROWS, Agnes, 1593
       wid. Humph. Androws
       Humph. Andrews, tailor and wf. Ag. take 2 appr. 23 Sept. 1565– 7
       July 1570
       will of Humph. Andrews Great Orphan Bk. vol. 1

25.   BARNES, David, 1593
       David Barnes, tucker/clothworker and wf. Joan take appr. 1 Oct.
       1579–20 Mar. 1581/2

28. CAROWE, Derby, 1593
    bur. 21 July 1593

30. COLLINS, Thomas, 1594
    burg. 3 Sept. 1572, freemason, fine 44s 6d.
    takes 2 appr. 2 Feb. 1572/3–23 June 1579
    bur. 13 Feb. 1593/4

31. COLWAYE, Owen, 1593
    bur. 26 Nov. 1593

32. DALLOWE, Thomas, 1593
    Thos. s.o. Andr. Dallowe of "Awdley", Salop, appr. Hen.
    Griffith, tailor and wf. Kath. 1 June 1570, 7 yrs.
    burg. 18 July 1580, appr. Hen. Griffith
    Thos. Dalloe, tailor, and wf. Joan take appr. John s.o. Thos.
    Paine of Credwell, Herefs. 3 Nov. 1585
    Wm. Askewe, appr., assigned to serve remainder of term of years
    unexpired with Thos. Dallowe, 30 Apr. 1585

33. DAVIES, Lewis, 1593
    Lewis Davies [no father] of co. Brecon, appr. to John Bawgh,
    turner, and wf. Alice 10 Feb. 1574/5, 7 yrs.
    burg. 30 June 1582, appr. John Baughe
    bur. 4 Sept. 1593

34. DAVIS, Thomas, 1594
    Thos. s.o. John Davis of Aylburton, Gloucs. appr. Leon.
    Sumpter, cooper and wf. Kath. 13 July 1570, 8 yrs.
    burg. 10 Feb. 1578/9, hooper, appr. Leon. Sumpter
    takes unnamed appr. 1 Sept. 1584
    bur. 7 Jan. 1593/4

36. ELLIOT, Christian, 1593
    bur. 4 Sept. 1593

38. FREELYNGE, Anne, 1593
    Paul Freling, goldsmith and wf. Anne take Garret Peter appr. 23
    Nov. 1553
    Cornelius Freling, goldsmith, burg. 28 Sept. 1562, s.o. Paul
    Freling
    Thos. s.o. Paul Freling, appr. to Anne Frelyng, wid. 14 Nov.
    1574, 7 yrs.

39. GOODYERE, Anthony, 1593
    ? Ant. Goodyere, tailor, and [? 1st.] wf. Elnr. take 2 appr. 11
    Dec. 1553–4 Feb. 1556/7

40. JAMES, John, 1593
     ? John s.o. John James of Bedminster appr. Hen. Davis, tucker
     and wf. Matilda 1 July 1559
     bur. 25 Nov. 1593

41. JONES, Thomas, 1593
     bur. 16 Nov. 1593

43. LAURENCE, George, 1593
     bur. 24 Oct. 1593

44. A PENDRYE, Gillian, 1593
     John Appenrye/Apenry shearman wf. and Gili—/Julian/Juliana
     take 4 appr. 10 June 1562–5 Nov. 1568
     bur. 23 Oct. 1593 "Gillin Pendery".

46. RISBY, Robert, 1593
     ? Robt. Risby, smith, and wf. Joan take appr Wm. s.o. Maur.
     Risby of Nympsfield, Gloucs. maltman 20 Dec. 1552, also Rich.
     Beylee 28 Jan. 1558/9
     ? Robt. Risby, smith, and Dor. [? 2nd] wf. take 2 appr. 10 Mar.–
     12 May 1571

47. ROBYNS, Nicholas, 1593
     Nich. Robyns of Bristol appr. father Nich. tailor, and wf. "Ame"
     23 Nov. 1570
     Nich. Robyns/Robins, tailor and wf. Amy/Amice/Anne take 9
     appr. 13 Feb. 1557/8–13 Mar. 1581/2

48. ROGERS, Thomas, 1593
     Thos. s.o. Rich. Rogers of Tenby, currier, appr. Thos. ap
     Gwillyam, tanner and wf. Alice 10 June 1536
     burg. 26 Aug. 1564 appr. Thos. "Agwillyam", tanner
     bur. 27 May 1593

50. SHORE, Richard, 1593
     burg. 19 Feb. 1577/8 yeoman, unspecified fine

51. TAWNYE, John, 1593
     John Tawnye, bowyer/roper and bowyer and wf. Kath. take 4
     appr. 9 June 1555–25 July 1579
     bur. 1 Nov. 1593

52. WILLIAMS, Richard, 1593
     ? burg. Rich. Williams, tucker, 27 Oct. 1576, appr. Edw.
     Robertes

53. BAYLIE als. PITTS, Agnes 1597/8
? Francis s.o. Rich. Bailie of Shifnal, Salop. appr. Hen. Beale 21
Jan. 1578/9
? burg. Francis Baylie 12 Nov. 1588 appr. Hen. Beale, tucker
? burg. Wm. Pytt, smith, 24 Sept. 1590, s.o. Rich. Pytt

55. BOYDELL, William, 1597
bur. 3 Dec. 1597

56. CICILL, Hugh, 1597
bur. 24 Apr. 1597

57. COOK, Roger, 1597
? Rog. Cooke, [no father] of Bristol appr. John Bushe, tanner, 30
Aug. 1570
? Rog. s.o. Hen. Cooke appr. David Harrys, tanner and wf. Joan,
1 Oct. 1570
burg. 26 Mar. 1571, tanner, s.o. Hen. Cook, tanner [entry deleted]
John s.o. Thos. Hunt of Westbury-on-Trym, husb. appr. Rog.
Cooke, tanner and wf. Eliz. 26 Nov. 1582
bur. 15 Dec. 1597

58. CORNISHE, Ralph, 1597
burg. 11 Sept. 1589, "Cornyshe", admitted "by consent of Robert
Kytchen, ald." and council

59. COULTON, John, 1597
John Coulton, whitawer/pointmaker and [? 1st.] wf. Joan take 3
appr. 9 May 1576–23 Nov. 1582

63. HANBYE, William, 1597
bur. 13 Apr. 1597 "son of William Hanby late deceased".

65. HUNT, John, 1597
John s.o. Thos. Hunt of Westbury-on-Trym, husb. appr. Rog.
Cooke, tanner and wf. Eliz. 26 Nov. 1582 7 yrs.
burg. 29 Nov. 1589, appr. Rog. Cooke, tanner

67. JOONS, Margaret, 1597
bur. 29 Nov. 1597

68. KNIGHT, John, 1597
Minor Canon, Bristol Cathedral, 1570
Curate St. Stephen, 1574
Possibly attended Cambridge or Oxford
wf. Christian bur. 22 July 1597
Volumes bequeathed:
Petrus Martinius *Grammatica Hebraea* edns. listed 1590 and 1597

Lambertus Danaeus *Commentarium in Prophetas Minores* Geneva 1586

Henry Smith: many works on gospels and epistles

Johannes Piscator: many works on gospels and epistles

Augustine Marlorat *A Catholike and ecclesiasticall exposition of S. Mathewe* 1569/70. STC 17404 [and of] *S. John* 1570/71 STC 17406

Heinrich Bullinger *Fiftie godlie and learned sermons divided into five decades, tr. out of Latine*, quarto, STC 4056

69.   MOWREY, Thomas, 1597
Morgan Jones s.o. John Morrye of Usk, Mons. appr. Thos Morrye, tailor [no wf.] 8 Mar. 1560/1
Thos. Morrye/Mory, tailor and wf. Margt. take 2 appr. 1 Nov. 1561–20 Apr. 1569

70.   NAYLER, Cicely, 1597
Edw. Nayler/Nailor, hooper and [? 1st] wf. Alice take 2 appr. 15 Jan. 1562/ 3–26 Aug. 1566
Edw. Naylor/Nailor, hooper and [? 2nd] wf. Cicely take 7 appr. 1 Dec. 1568–19 May 1583
bur. 29 Aug. 1597 "Sisly"

71.   NICHOLLS, Edward, 1597
Edw. s.o. Rich. Nicholles of Ross, Herefs. appr. Edw. French, grocer and wf. Anne, 20 May 1573, 7 yrs
burg. 14 Feb. 1580/1, appr. Edw. French, grocer, decd.
Wm. s.o. Wm Gurney of Cirencester appr. Edw. Nicholles, grocer 25 June 1583
bur. 25 June 1597

72.   OLDFYLDE, Mary, 1597
bur. 1 Oct. 1597 "sister of Maude Tyther"

73.   POPLEY, Edmund, 1597
burg. 17 June 1578, girdler, s.o. John Popley, hooper
bur. 14 June 1597

74.   POWELL, John, 1597
burg. 27 July 1570, m. Alborowgh, wid. of Rich. Sarches
John Powell, shoemaker and wf. Alborowe/Albrogh/Albero/ Albough take 4 appr. 5 Aug. 1572–25 July 1585

75.   RIDER, Thomas, 1597
bur. 30 Apr. 1597 "mynister of Redcliffe"

77.   SYMONS, Joan, 1597
burg. Thos. Symons, jun. merchant 12 Sept. 1580, s.o. Thos. Symons, merchant
bur. 8 Sept. 1597

79. VINCENT, John, 1597
     John s.o. Thos. Vynsent of Bathford, Som. appr. Math. Nede,
     joiner and wf. Alice, 6 Feb. 1572/3
     bur. 22 June 1597 "Vinson"

81. WESTACOTT, Richard, 1597
     burg. "Westkott", no occup., 5 Aug. 1586, m. d. o. John Baily

82. WHITEHEAD, Peter, 1597
     burg. 4 Nov. 1592, m. wid. Anth. Raye

84. YOUNGE, Margaret, 1597
     bur. 31 Mar. 1597

85. BURGES, Robert, 1598
     burg. 7 Oct. 1594, butcher, appr. Chris Galloway
     bur. 28 Feb. 1598/9

86. BURGES, Sampson, 1598
     burg. 8 July 1588, appr. John Burgis, hatmaker
     bur. 19 Feb. 1597/8

87. BURNETT, Joan, 1598
     Wm. Burnett/Burnard, cardmaker and wf. Margt. take 6 appr. 10
     June 1567–6 Dec. 1577.
     Wm. Burnett [no wf.] takes appr. 7 Oct. 1578.
     Wm. Burnett, cardmaker and wf. Joan take 4 appr. 23 Nov.
     1582–20 May 1585

88. COOPER, Richard, 1598
     Rich. s.o. Ancel Cooper of Ashford, Salop. appr. Edm. Robertes,
     tucker and wf. Joan, 12 Aug. 1578, 7 yrs.

89. EDWARDS, Edmund, 1598
     ? burg. 14 May 1597, baker, appr. of father Sampson Edwards
     Sampson Edwards, baker and wf. Edith take 4 appr. 22 June
     1577–10 Feb. 1585/6

91. GARRETT, Robert, 1598
     ? burg. Robt. Gerratt, carpenter, 16 Sept. 1573, m. Margt. d.o.
     Rog. Marwell

92. GOODMAN, Thomas, 1598
     burg. 17 Sept. 1562, m. Matilda d.o. Rog. Aprichard, ? weaver
     Thos. Goodman, joiner and wf. Maud take 3 appr. 19 Sept.
     1567–3 Nov. 1572

93.   GOSNELL, Julian, 1598
Alan, s.o. Yeaman Gozenell of Bridgenorth, Salop, tailor, appr.
Wm. Glasberrow, pewterer and wf. Margt. 11 July 1539
Alan Gosnell, pewterer and wf. Julia/Julian/Juliana take 4 appr. 8
June 1553–8 May 1569

95.   HAYWARD, Thomas, 1598
Thos. s.o. Wm. Haward of Little Wenlock, Salop. appr. Thos.
Grene, sherman and wf. Kath. 31 Jan. 1571/2, 7 yrs.
burg. Thos. Hawarde, 1 Dec. 1579, appr. Thos. Grene, sherman,
and after his death to wid. Kath.

98.   LEY, John, 1598
bur. 7 Sept. 1598, haulier

100.   MANNINGE, Richard, 1598
bur. 10 Feb. 1598/9

102.   SETTLE, Thomas, 1598
? Thos. Settle, turner and wf. Kath. take 2 appr. 9 Nov. 1565–1
Nov. 1566
? Thos. Settle, turner and wf. Maud/Matilda/Magdalen take 4
appr. 26 Mar. 1574–11 May 1585 [? Margt. 3rd wf.]
bur. 27 Dec. 1598

103.   SMITH, Richard, 1598
? Rich. Smith, shearman and wf. Margt. take 5 appr. 20 Nov.
1573–1 May 1585 [? Elnr. 2nd wf.]

104.   WOODNEY, William, 1598
? burg. Wm. Woodnet, 22 Mar. 1594/5, appr. John Jacob, pointmaker
bur. 26 Feb. 1598/9 "Woodnie"

105.   WRIGHT, Margery, 1598
? Ralph Wryte burg. 13 Oct. 1587, appr. Erasmus Wryte
bur. 23 Jan. 1597/8

107.   BANTONN, Elizabeth, 1599
? Mich. Burgende, appr. John Banting, mercer and wf. Eliz. 5
Dec. 1563
bur. *c*. 15 June 1599

109.   BUTLER, William, 1599
bur. 20 Apr. 1599

110.   CHAMBERS, Alice, 1599
bur. 2 Apr. 1599

111.   COOCKE, John, 1599
? John s.o. Thos. Cooke of Habberley, Worcs., husb. appr. Wm.
Dane, weaver and wf. Eve, 1 Sept. 1554, 8 yrs.
? burg. John Coke, 2 Jan. 1565/6, appr. Wm. Dane, weaver
John Cooke, weaver and wf. Anne/Agnes take 5 appr. 11 Feb.
1565/6–10 Aug. 1579
bur. 5 June 1599

112.   CORYE, Robert, 1599/1600
? Robt. s.o. Robt. Corie of Barton nr. Bristol, appr. John
Kytchyn, shoemaker and wf. Edith, 1 Nov. 1568
? John, s.o. Robt. Corye of Barton nr. Bristol, husb. appr. Rich.
Clarke and wf. Alice, 17 Oct. 1575
? Thos. s.o. Robt. Cory of Barton Regis, appr. John Barry, smith
and wf. Margy. 1 Nov. 1579
bur. 29 Jan. 1599/1600

113.   DURAND, Morris, 1599/1600
Curate, St. Ewen, 1574, and a fortnight's service there 1579–80,
prob. Cambridge graduate therefore former Dominican friar

115.   GLEWE, Richard, 1599
burg. 31 July 1593, sailor, m. wid. Thos. Sharpe, sailor
bur. 8 Aug. 1599

119.   LANGTON, Margaret, 1599
? John s.o. John Mynyfe of Honiton, appr. Rich. Langton, notary
public, and wf. Margt. 1 Oct. 1578

121.   MASONE, Agnes, 1599
see Thos. Masson

122.   MASSON/MASON, Thomas, 1599
burg. 14 Jan 1557/8, appr. John Corfell, baker
memo. 31 Jan. 1557/8 Robt. Sowthall and Wm. Awste, master
bakers, presented Thos. Mason as fit to carry on trade of baker,
under sign illustr. in margin
Thos. Mason, baker and wf. Ag. take 6 appr. 27 Apr. 1559–1
May 1576
bur. 3 Oct. 1599

123.   NEWTONN, James, 1599/1600
Jas. s.o. David Nuton of Bristol, shearman appr. Robt.
Nicholson, tailor and wf. Eliz. 18 May 1566, 12 yrs.
burg. 19 Mar. 1577/8, appr. Robt. Nicholson, tailor
Jas. Newton, tailor and wf. Joan take 3 appr. 30 June 1578–24
Dec. 1585

124. PACKER, William, 1599
     bur. 10 June 1599

125. PANTHURE, Arthur, 1599
     burg. 26 Oct. 1581, yeoman, m. Anne one of d. of John Merick,
     skinner
     John s.o. Rich. White of Waterford, Ireland, appr. Arth. Panter,
     merchant and wf. Anne, 25 July 1585

126. ROTHELL, John, 1599
     ? John Rothell of Newbury, appr. John Stones, brewer and wf.
     Joan, 12 May 1567, 7 Yrs.
     burg. 8 Jan. 1573/4, brewer, m. Eliz. d.o. John White, shoemaker
     John Rothell, brewer and wf. Eliz. take 3 appr. 8 Aug. 1575–1
     Mar. 1584/5 [? Alice 2nd wf.]
     bur. 24 Aug. 1599

127. SIMONS, Alice, 1599
     ? John Simmons/Symons, spurrier and wf. Alice take 3 appr. 12
     July 1553–5 Mar. 1567/8

128. TAYLOR, James, 1599
     Jas. s.o. Wm. Tailor of Barton Hundred, appr. John Barnes, tucker
     and wf. Joan, 1 Feb. 1559/60
     burg. 23 Aug. 1576, appr. John Barnes, sen.
     Jas. Tailor/Tayler/Taylor, tucker and wf. Alice take 4 appr. 19
     Dec. 1578–21 Oct. 1585

131. WINCHOMBE, John, 1599
     bur. 24 Nov. 1599

132. ADEANE, John, 1600
     John s.o. John Adeane of Awre, Gloucs. decd. appr. Andr. Yate,
     30 Sept. 1582, 7 yrs.
     burg. 8 May 1595, appr. Andr. Yate, soapmaker and chandler

133. AUFLITT, Edmund, 1600
     Sim. s.o. Sim. Alflat of Burford, Oxon. appr. "Ed." Alflat, soap-
     maker, 15 July 1580, 8 yrs.
     bur. 28 June 1600 "Alslett"

134. BEESE, Thomas, 1600
     Thos. s.o. Thos. Bees of "Lemsome" [no county] appr. Robt.
     Williams, tucker and wf. Joan, 1 Dec. 1578
     burg. 14 Aug. 1588, appr. Robt. Williams, tucker

136. BUSHE, Thomas, 1600/1601
     burg. 18 Oct. 1590, appr. John Bushe, tanner

137.   BYRDE, John, 1600/1601
John s.o. Wm. Birde of Dundry, Som. appr. Hugh Bache, shearman
and wf. Ag. 31 Mar. 1579, 8 yrs.
burg. 18 June 1588, appr. Hugh Bache, shearman

138.   DITTIE, Anthony, 1600
Anth. s.o. Rich. Dittie of "Soteholwaie" Som. appr. Hen. Dittie,
musician and wf. Alice, 20 Apr. 1581
Hen. Dittye, musician, burg. 18 Jan. 1580/1. fine 53s 4d
Anth. Dittie, burg. 1 July 1590, appr. Hen. Dyttye, musician

139.   HENDLYE, Roger, 1600
bur. 12 Aug. 1600 "Henlie"

141.   MORRICE, Nicholas, 1600
burg. Nich. Mores, sailor, 28 Feb. 1598/9, m. Anne d.o. John
Boydell

142.   NICHOLAS, William, 1600
burg. 15 July 1572, m. Margy. d.o. Edw. Mylles, pointmaker,
decd.
bur. 14 Dec. 1600 "Nickles"

143.   POPE, Robert, 1600
bur. 1 Feb. 1599/1600

144.   POYNER, Clemence, 1600/1
? John s.o. Thos. Clerk, appr. Barth. Poynard, mercer and wf.
Clementine, 13 Apr. 1556
bur. 4 Dec. 1600, All Saints, "widow, of the parish of st. Ewen"

145.   WHITE, Patrick, 1600
bur. 14 May 1600, Redcliffe

146.   WIDGINS/WIGGINS, William, 1600
burg. Wm. Wiggyns, capper, 24 July 1572, s.o. John Wiggyns,
capper
? Mich. s.o. John Wygons, capper, appr. Wm. Atkyns, hooper
and wf. Kath. 14 Oct. 1535

148.   WOULFE, Nicholas, 1600
Nich. Woolf, joiner and wf. Kath. take 9 appr. 17 Apr. 1557–2
Oct. 1582
bur. 16 Nov. 1600

149.   YEMAN, John, 1600
burg. 5 Dec. 1590, appr. Wm. Yeman, grocer, decd.
bur. 13 July 1600 "Yemans"

150.   ANDROWES, Melchisedich, 1601
         s.o. Geo. Andrewes/Androwes of Bideford, Devon
         appr. of Robt. Rogers, soapmaker and chandler and wf. Elnr.
         Robt. Rogers burg. 29 Nov. 1585, s.o. Rich. Rogers, soapmaker
         bur. 4 Feb. 1600/1, Redcliffe, "Myles Chesticke Andrew serv."

152.   AWSTINE, William, 1601
         burg. Wm. Austen 25 Jan. 1596/7, appr. Hen. Drewet, pinner

154.   BURTTE, William, 1601
         Wm. s.o. Wm. Birte, tailor, appr. Edw. Naylor, hooper and wf.
         Alice, 15 Jan. 1561/2, 7 yrs.
         Wm. Byrt burg. 18 Jan. 1569/70, appr. Edw. Nailor, hooper
         Wm. Burt (e), hooper and wf. Joan take 2 appr. 28 June 1581–28
         Mar. 1584

156.   FLEMING, Thomas, 1601/2
         burg. 22 Feb. 1579/80, appr. John Parthop, then appr. Wm. Yate,
         soapmaker and chandler

157.   HAWLE, Richard, 1601
         bur. 12 Mar. 1600/1

158.   JOHNES, James, 1601
         Jas. s.o. Geo. Jones of Llanbadoc, Mons. appr. John Barowe,
         shearman and wf. Anne, 1 May 1574, 8 yrs.
         burg. Jas. Jones 7 Oct. 1581, appr. John Barrs, shearman
         Jas. Jones, shearman and wf. Margy/Margt take 2 appr. 4 Oct.
         1585–22 Apr. 1586

160.   PITTES, John, 1601
         bur. Margt. wf. of Mr. John Pittes, 16 Sept. 1593
         bur. John Pittes 27 Feb. 1600/1

162.   STAPLE, John, 1601
         burg. 27 Feb. 1577/8, "furber", m. Matilda d.o. Thos. Whitby
         John Staple, armourer and wf. Anne take 2 appr. 24 Dec.
         1580–25 Jan 1582/ 3
         bur. 15 Sept. 1601

163.   WILLIAMS, David, 1601/2
         David s.o. Wm. Howell of Aberguyte, Carm. appr. Math. Nede,
         joiner and wf. Alice, 1 June 1581, 7 yrs.
         burg. 15 Oct. 1588, appr. Math. Nede

165.   ALDWORTH, Thomas, 1602
         burg. 6 Feb. 1576/7, hooper, appr. Eliz. Aldworth
         Thos. Aldworth, hooper, takes 2 appr. 10 Aug. 1583–30 Sept.
         1584
         Thos. Aldworth, hooper and wf. Mary take appr. 29 Sept. 1583

166.   BARWELL, Thomas, 1602
       burg. 11 May 1565, appr. Thos. Crickeland, tucker
       Thos. Barwell, tucker and wf. Eliz. take 4 appr. 30 July 1567–6
       June 1573 [? Joan 2nd wf.]

167.   BATTIN, Jervis, 1602/3
       burg. 16 Aug. 1592, m. Eliz. wid. Thos. Woodforde
       bur. 9 Jan. 1602/3

168.   BONNER, Joan, 1602
       John s.o. Wm. Bonor of Hungerford, Berks. shearman appr. Hen.
       Walton, cardmaker and wf. Alice, 12 Aug. 1547
       John Bonner, cardmaker and wf. Joan take 6 appr. 8 Aug. 1559–
       1 Oct. 1568
       bur. 3 June 1602

169.   CHAUNDLER, Margaret, 1602
       Robt. s.o. Phil. Chaunler of Tewkesbury appr. Humph. Clovill,
       goldsmith and wf. Anne, Sept. 1 1574

170.   CLARKE, John, 1602
       ? John Clarke burg. 23 Oct. 1566, appr. Rich. Clarke, whitawer
       John Clark, pointmaker and wf. Alice take appr. 1 Nov. 1583

171.   CROUCHINGTONN, William, 1602
       bur. 22 Mar. 1601/2 "Crowthington"

172.   DAVIES, Alice, 1602/3
       John Davis burg. 20 Apr. 1564, appr. John Thomas, hooper
       John Davis, hooper and wf. Alice take appr. 26 July 1577

175.   GRAYE, John, 1602
       ? John Grey burg. 23 Oct. 1578, appr. Ralph Hassold, tucker
       ? John Gray, clothier, takes appr. 14 Nov. 1581
       ? John Gray, tucker and wf. Flor. take appr. 9 Mar. 1584/5

177.   KEMBLE, Mary, 1602/3
       Wm. Stybbes, yeoman. burg. 4 Sept. 1570, fine 44s 6d

181.   STONES, John, 1602
       bur. 4 June 1602

183.   TYPPETT, John, 1602
       bur. 7 Apr. 1602

184.   WALLIS, John, 1602
       bur. 6 July 1602 "Willis"

185. WELSHE, Richard, 1602/3
     burg. 11 Feb. 1580/1, m. "Elizabeth Rudge tailor formerly
     burgess" [? name of her previous husband omitted]
     Rich. Welche/Welsh, tailor and wf. Eliz. take 2 appr. 12 June
     1581–5 Aug. 1585

188. HARTE, David, 1559
     David Hart/Harte, shearman and wf. Margt., take 5 appr. 16 Jan.
     1535/6–13 Apr. 1555
     Thos. s.o. David Harte, shearman, appr. Robt. Durban, merchant
     and wf. Edith, 12 July 1540, 13 yrs.

189. HARTE, William, 1559
     ? Wm. Hart, baker and [? 1st] wf. Alice take 2 appr. 7 Aug.
     1539–25 June 1540
     Wm. s.o. Thos. Harte late of Bristol, baker, appr. Wm. Harte [no
     trade] and wf. Kath. 5 May 1553
     Wm. Harte, baker and wf. Kath. take appr. 12 Mar. 1556/7

191. MORSE, Richard, 1559
     ? Rich. Morse, baker and wf. Agatha take appr. 18 Mar. 1555/6
     ? Rich. Morse [no trade] and wf. Agnes take appr. 6 Aug. 1556

GLOSSARY

A Note on Sources used in compiling the Glossary.

Most words have been defined from the *Shorter Oxford English Dictionary* and the spellings given therein have been adopted as standard. Reference has also been made to the *Oxford English Dictionary*, to *Clifton and Westbury Probate Inventories* (A.L.H.A.) by John S. Moore and also to his *The Goods and Chattels of Our Forefathers* (Phillimore), to *A Glossary of Household, Farming and Trade Terms from Probate Inventories*, (Derbyshire Record Society) by Rosemary Milward and to the Essex Record Office publications *Elizabethan Life*, by F.G. Emmison and *Farm and Cottage Inventories* by F.W. Steer as well as *The Cloth Industry in the West of England* (Alan Sutton) by J. de L. Mann and J.O. Halliwell's *Dictionary of Archaic and Provincial Words* (1847).

andirons [178] a pair of horizontal bars, on short feet with upright pillars, placed at each side of the hearth to support burning wood
angel [50] gold coin deriving its name from the effigy of the Archangel Michael
antic [5] a monstrous, fantastic or incongruous representation of objects of the animal or vegetable kingdom
apparel [passim] personal outfit or attire; clothing
arras [107] [134] rich tapestry fabric in which figures and scenes are woven in colours
"ayethe" see *eythe*
baize [119] a coarse woollen stuff having a long nap
band [178] collar or ruff
beads, pair of [1] rosary
bedcase [56] possibly a bedstead but more probably a cover for the featherbed; a mattress cover
bell candlestick [37] with bell-shaped base, or perhaps, made of bell-metal
boards [18] market stall or pavement space with right to trade
bow buttons [108] possibly of a bent or curved shape or perhaps made at Bow in London

breeches [34] [56] a garment covering the loins and thighs

broach [1] [106] a spit

"broke" [172] brooch; meaning included necklace and bracelet as well as
ornamental pin

Bruges satin [1] presumably from Bruges and hence indicative of the type
and quality

budge [5] [172] a kind of fur consisting of lamb's skin with the wool
dressed outwards

bulk [166] a framework projecting from the front of a shop

bushel [107] a measure of capacity containing 4 pecks or 8 gallons

buskins [56] covering for the foot or leg reaching to the calf or knee

calico [102] [107] cotton cloth imported from the east

cambric [45] a kind of fine white linen

camlet [192] originally a costly eastern fabric, subsequently substitutes for
the same, of wool, silk, linen etc.

cardmaker [5] one who makes cards for combing wool

cassock [10] a long, loose coat or gown

cathern [86] [91] form of "cauldron" [*see below*]

cauldron [106] a large kettle or boiler

"chaffen" [30] for *chafing-dish* [q.v.]

chafing-dish [56] [102] [106] a vessel to hold burning fuel for heating
anything placed upon it

"chafron" [1] for *chafing-dish* [q.v.]

chandling [155] candle-making

chapman, petty [28] a retail dealer, hawker, pedlar

charger [60] [86] large plate or flat dish

childbed clothes [134] [137] fine quality bed-linen [see 187]

chilver [131] a ewe-lamb

"clave" [135] possibly cloth [Moore note forms "clath" and "clove"; see
also *handles, pairs of*, below]

cleave [56] probably a cleaver

"cobert" cloth [187] for cupboard cloth; the original cupboard was simply
a board suported by legs and covered with a cloth or carpet on which
household plate, especially drinking cups, was placed

cock-loft [119] a small upper loft, usually reached by a ladder

coffer [36] [84] a strong box in which money or valuables are kept

"cofferen" [105] probably for coffer

"colbert" [45] probably for cupboard

cotton [134] a woollen fabric of the nature of frieze

counter [50] table or desk for counting money

covenant year a further year's work agreed to be undertaken for master
after completion of term of appenticeship

coverlet [41] the uppermost covering for a bed

crock [3] [20] [28] [36] earthenware or metal pot

croft [166] piece of enclosed ground

cruse [56] [171] [175] a pot, jar or bottle

Dansk chest [149] Dansk = Danish

diaper [1] a linen fabric woven with a small and simple pattern, formed by the different directions of the thread

dirige [1] form of *dirge*: in the Latin rite the first word of the antiphon at Matins in the office of the Dead, used as a name for that service

doublet [1] [34] [56] a close-fitting body garment worn by men

dowlas [106] a kind of linen

ell [45] a measure of length, being 45 inches

engrain [108] dye crimson or scarlet with cochineal

ewer [28] a pitcher with a wide spout, used to bring water for washing

eythe [99] a harrow

firm [27] as noun, signature; as verb, to make a document valid by seal, signature or the like

flannen [37] original form of the word flannel, which is an open woollen stuff of loose texture

flask [94] [142] a case of leather, metal or horn to carry gunpowder in

flock a material consisting of the coarse tufts and refuse of wool or cotton . . . used for stuffing beds, cushions, mattresses etc.

flock-bed [30] [34] [41] [166] [137] one stuffed with flock

forest bill [56] bill-hook; presumably differing from the hedge-bill

french bedstead [164] presumably of a type used in, or imported from, France

frieze [11] [82] [148] a kind of coarse woollen cloth with a nap, usually on one side only

frizado [119] a fine kind of frieze

furber [162] form of "furbisher": one who removed rust from weapons, armour etc. burnishes and polishes them

fustian [187] cloth with a linen warp and a cotton weft

garnish [187] a set of vessels for table use especially of pewter

gimmals [92] hinges

goblet [15] [24] a drinking-cup, bowl shaped and without handles, sometimes mounted on a foot and fitted with a cover

gorget [187] an article of female dress, covering the neck and breast

gossip [129] a god-parent

grogram [80] a coarse fabric of silk, of mohair and wool or of these mixed with silk, often stiffened with gum

gridiron [45] a framework of parallel metal bars, used for broiling meat or fish over a fire

halberd [172] a military weapon, a kind of combination between a spear and a battle-axe

half a crown [106] coin worth 2 shillings and six pence

halfendeal [81] the half-part

halfhead bedstead [56] [148] [137] bedstead with short corner-posts without canopies

hallier [5] haulier; one who hauls

handles, pairs of [135] holders for teazel-heads used by shearmen to finish cloth [Emmison noted examples in Essex]

hard beasts [85] barren beasts [but Halliwell gives the meaning "full grown"]

head napkin [82] head-scarf

hogshead [185] a large cask for liquids, capacity varying for different liquids

holland [45] a linen fabric, so called because the Low Countries were particularly suited to the growth of flax from which high-quality linen could be produced

hose [1] clothing for the leg, sometimes also covering the foot

hurden [107] [176] coarse flaxen cloth

hurds [105] the coarser parts of flax or hemp

Irish rug [70] [144] type of rug [q.v.] presumably made of wool imported from Ireland

"jangler" for *jingle*, a jingling bell [1]

jerkin [14] a close-fitting jacket or short coat, often made of leather

joined bedstead [34] [46] bedstead with all joints made with mortice and tenon joints, made by a carpenter and superior to pegged joints

journeyman [135] one who having completed his apprenticeship to a trade, is qualified to work at it for day's wages

"kalikeene" [45] possibly for *cameline*, a kind of cloth supposed to be made of camel's hair

kerchief [82] a cloth used to cover the head

kersey [135] a kind of coarse, narrow cloth, woven from long wool and usually ribbed

"kever" for *cover* [15]

"kinderkin" [147] form of *kilderkin* a cask for liquids holding 16 to 18 gallons

latten [178] a mixed metal of yellow colour, either identical with or very like brass

limbeck [83] a still for making liquor

lye [166] a mixture of ashes and water for washing and scouring

mantle [30] a loose, sleeveless cloak

medley cloth [45] [119] cloth woven with wools of different colours or shades

mind [1] the commemoration of a departed soul especially by a requiem on the day of the funeral in any month or year following

mockado [45] a kind of cloth much used for clothing in 16th and 17th centuries

noble [96] a gold coin, value 6s 8d

nuncupative [26] of will, oral

"offras" [1] for *orfray* (in Middle English "orfreis") rich embroidery, often gold, on ecclesiastical vestment

orchel maker (4 note] a maker of orchell or orchil, a red or violet dye prepared from lichens

paned [97] made of strips of different coloured cloth joined together

partlet [82] [107] an article of apparel worn about the neck and upper part of the chest, chiefly by women: a collar or ruff

"payse" [99] a weight, commonly found as *cheese paise* for weighing cheese

petronel [94] a large pistol, used especially by horse-soldiers

pillow-bere [56] [60] [102] [107] [159] [176] pillowcase

platter [36] a flat dish or plate for food

pointmaker [15] [17] maker of tagged lace or cord for attaching hose to doublet or for lacing a bodice

pole-axe [164] a halberd or the like carried by the bodyguard of a great personage

posnet [188] a small metal pot for boiling, having a handle and three feet

pottage [149] soup, especially a thick soup

pottinger [56] a vessel of metal, earthenware or wood for holding soup, broth etc.

pottle [102] a measure of capacity equal to half a gallon

pottle pot [83] a drinking vessel holding a pottle or two quarts "poulte" [122]

"poulte" [122] probably for *poultz*: peas and beans

powdering tub [166] a tub for salting meat

present pots [45] possibly pots kept ready to hand

"prise pot" [187] ?perhaps one kept for its intrinsic value as an investment

puke [5] a superior kind of woollen cloth of which gowns were made

quarrel [192] a small heavy arrow or bolt used with a cross-bow

racks [175] frames upon which cloth is stretched

relict [passim] widow

rough layer [30] rough mason, building only with unhewn stone

rug [30] a rough woollen material, a sort of coarse frieze

russel [1] a kind of woollen fabric

russet [6] [82] a coarse home-spun cloth of a reddish-brown, grey or neutral colour

"rygoled" [91] perhaps meaning decorated with grooves from *rigol*, a groove or small channel

salt [70] salt-cellar

saucer [36] a dish or deep plate in which salt or sauces were placed upon the table

say [1] a cloth of fine texture resembling serge

settle [166] a long wooden bench or a ledge

shepton colour [172] the production of coloured cloth, dyed in the wool, was carried out at Shepton Mallet, Som.

shippon [99] cattle-shed

skillet [102] a cooking utensil usually having three or four feet and a long handle, used for boiling liquids etc.

skimmer [56] a shallow utensil, usually perforated, employed in skimming liquids

smock [70] [107] a woman's undergarment, a shift

"sollowe" [50] for *sullow* a plough

spanish cushions [102] probably covered with spanish leather

spruce [105] [148] bought or obtained from Prussia – sometimes implying "made of spruce fir"

stained cloth [56] [63] a painted cloth used as a wall-hanging, being cheaper than tapestry

stammel [178] a coarse woollen cloth or linsey-woolsey usually dyed red, or as a colour, the shade of red in which the cloth was commonly dyed

standards [24] permanent or necessary furniture of apparatus

standing bedstead [119] [137] joined bedstead, either four posted or half-headed, as opposed to moveable truckle bed [q.v.]

stoned [143] not castrated

surplice [1] a loose vestment of white linen worn by clerics

tallet [99] hay-loft formed by boarding joists over stable and, by extension, fodder stored there

taster [172] a small shallow cup of silver for tasting wines

tawny [172] a shade of brown

tester [166] a canopy over a bed, supported on the posts of the bedstead

tissue [1] a rich kind of cloth, often interwoven with gold and silver

touchbox [94] [142] a box for touch-powder or priming-powder, part of a musketeer's equipment

trencher [56] a flat piece of wood on which meat was served and cut up; a plate or platter

"trendle" [179] for *truckle*

trough [166] narrow, open vessel to contain liquid

"trowe" [102] form of *trough* [*see above*]

truckle bed [3] [148] low bed on castors, usually kept under a standing bedstead during the day

truss [35] a bundle of hay or straw

tucker [135] a fuller, a cloth-finisher

"viadge" [70] not traced but "viage" is obsolete form of "voyage" which itself could mean transit or passage, possibly becoming a burgess was viewed in this way

voider [83] a tray for clearing dirty plates and uneaten food from tables

wain [50] a farm-cart, usually four-wheeled, with four sides or no sides at all

wall plates [166] a horizontal timber at the top or bottom of a framing

wainscot [24] [46] [99] [109] [148] panel-work of oak or other wood, lining or used to line the walls of a room

whittawer [59] one who taws (prepares or dresses) skins into white leather

withy [135] a flexible branch or a willow used for tying or binding

worsted [1] [148] a woollen fabric or stuff made from well-twisted yarn

"yower" for *ewer* [28] [q.v.]

INDEXES

[Note: numbers given are those of the wills, not pages. Items shown in italics relate to material additional to that in the will appearing only in the related biographical note.]

INDEX OF PERSONAL NAMES

—LLYN [blank] 61
—SON, John 152
—TYNNE, Joan 83
[blank], Alice 10; Alses 107; Anne 115, 165,
    187; David 152; Edith 187; Edw. 8; Ellen
    139; Francis 96; Jane 114; John 73; Kath.
    10; Margt. 35; Margy. 67, 139, 160; Rich.
    1; Thos. 10; Sibyl 187

A PENDRYE (APPENDRY; *AP(P)ENRY(E);
    PENDERY*), Ann 44; Gillian/*Julian* 44;
    Joan 44; *John* 44
ABBINTON, Elnr. 78, 83
ABEVAN, Wm. 4
ABLLE, John 115
ABRAHAM, Wm. 36
AD(D)AMS, Ann 70; Dan. 70; Eliz. 37; Joan
    37; John 15; Nich. 65; Thos. 70
ADEANE (DEANE), Ann 132; Elnr. 132;
    Jane 132; John 132; *John (sen.) 132*;
    Kath. 132; Mary 132; Math. 132; Robt.
    37, 132, 153; Robt. (jun.) 132; Thos. 132
AGROVE, Rich. 99
AISHOLENT, John 112
ALDWORTH, [blank] 105; *Eliz. 165*;
    Erasmus 165; John 105, 113; *Mary 165*;
    Robt. 105, 113, 165, Thos. 105, 165
ALFORD, Wm. 89
AMTILL, Robt. 61
ANDROW(E)S *(ANDREWES)*, Abigail 24;
    Ag. 24; Ann 24; *Geo. 150*; Humph. 24;
    Humph. (jun.) 24; Jane 150; John 24;
    Melchisedich 150; Susan 150
ANEWLEY (ANULEY), Edm. 83; Joan 83
*AP GWILLYAM (AGWILLYAM), Alice 48;
    Thos. 48*
APOWELL, Edw. 5; Kath. 5; Mary 5
APPRICE, Alice 106; John 106; Wm. 20
APPULTON, Hen. 142
APRICHARD, Matilda 92; Rog. 92
ARCHELL, Mr. 192

ARNOLDE, Nich. 187
ARTHUR, Mr. 96; Rich. 47, 94, 120
ARUND(E)L(E), Frances/Francis 96
ASH(E)HURST(E) (AISH(E)HURST;
    AYSHEHURST(E)), Alice 106; Arthur
    106; Joan 106; John 106, 131; Rich. 3;
    Susanna 106; Thos. 106; Wm. 106
ASHLIN, Thos. 106
ASKEWE, Wm. 32
ATKINS (ATKYNS), John 68; *Kath 146*;
    Wm. 70, 92, 102, *146*, 154, 185
AUFLITT als. ALFLATT *(ALFLAT;
    ALSLETT)*, Ag. 133; Ag. (jun.) 133;
    Cic. 133; Edm. 133; Edm. (jun.) 133;
    Joan 133; Margy. 133; *Sim. (jun. and
    sen.) 133*
AUSTINE *(AUSTEN;* AWSTINE), Kath.
    152; Wm. 152
AVERY, Alice 151; Edw. 151; Fortune
    151; John 35, 151
AWBRYE, Lewis 39
AWNDD, John 1; Thos. 1
AWSTE, Wm. 122
AYSHEKENE, Thos. 131
AYTON, Rich. 179

BABB(E), Wm. 1
BACHE, Ag. 137; Hugh 137
BADEYERE, Nich. 17
BAKER, Edw. 64, 92; Hen. 142
BALDWIN, Geo. 169
BALTON, Walt. 158
BANTON(N) *(BANTINGE)*, David 107;
    Eliz. 107; Jas. 107; *John 107*
BANY, Jane 97
BARBOUR, Jas. 85
BARKELEY see BERKELEY
BARNES, Clement 66; David 25; Joan 25,
    128; John 25, *128*; Wm. 25, 134
BARNET (BARNATT), Ann 153; Eliz.
    153; John 70

BARNSLEY, Margy. 172; Nich. 172
BARNYS, Maud 115
BAROWE, Ann 158; John 158
BARRS John 158
BARRY, *John 112; Margy. 112*; Thos. 189
BARWELL, Ag. 166; *Eliz. 166*; Joan 166;
    Jonas 166; Thos. 166; Wm. 166
BARWICKE, Rich. 7
BATT, Rich. 135
BAT(T)EN (BATTIN), Alice 26; Eliz. 167;
    Jervis 167; John 26; Mary 26; Maurice
    1; Sim. 30, 63, 179; Thos. 49
BAUGHE (BAWGH), Alice 33; John 33
BAYLIE als. PITTS, Ag. 53
BAYLY(E) (BAILY(E); BALYE; BAY-
    LEY; BAYLIE; *BEYLEE*), Eliz. 73;
    Francis 53; Nich. 54; Rich. *46, 53*, 88,
    135, 166, 185; Thos. 54
BAYMART, Alex. 161
BAYNARD, Thos. 100, 112, 151
BAYNEHAM, Robt. 186
BEAKE, John 106
BEALE, Hen. 53
BECK*(E)*, Joan 9; *John 9*
BEES*(E)*, Ellen 134; John 134; Margt. 134;
    Martha 134; Thos. 25, 134; *Thos. (sen.)
    134*
BELBIN, Jas. 150
BELCHER (BELSHERE), Joan 108, 119;
    Toby 108, 119; Walt. 108
BELL, John 15
BELLEMAN, Jas. 76
BENBOWE, [blank] 35; Wm. 191
BENNE, Wm. 28, 48
BENNET (BENETT), Robt. 91; Thos. 92
BERKEL(E)Y (BARKELY; BARKLEY;
    BERKLEY), Ann 187; Cic. 187; Edw.
    187; Elnr. 187; Frances 187; Maurice
    187; Siball 187
BERRET, John 118
BESER, Joan 174; Rich. 174; Robt. 174;
    Thompson 174
BETTS, Welthian 5
BEYMAND, Harry 27; Joan 27
BIGGS, Emanuel 111
BILLING (BYLLYNG), Elnr. 97; Rich. 97,
    174
BIRDE see BYRDE
BIRKEN (BIRKIN; BYRKIN), Ann 153;
    Anth. 153; Geo. 153; Jas. 153; Joan
    153; John 132, 153; Margt. 132; Math.
    153; Rich. 153; Thos. 153; Wm. 153
BISHOPPE (BISSHOP; BYSHOPPE;
    BYSS(H)OP), Thos. 44, 111, 128; Wm.
    61, 109
BISTAN, Jas. 149
BLAKE, Alex. 28; Phil. 28
BLUNDYE, John 32; Margy. 32; Mary 32;
    Rich. 32; Rich. (jun.) 32

BOLDWIN, wid. 107
BOLWELL, John 30
BONNDE, [blank] 70; Geo. 70; Thos. 70
BONNER *(BONOR)*, Joan 168; John 5;
    Wm. 168
BOORD, Wm. 175
BORGES, Samson 48
BOROWES, John 1
BOSDEN, Edw. 64, 145, 182
BOSWELL (BOSWALL), Ann 115; Rich. 61
BOULTON (BOWLTON), John 96, 171
BOVYE, John 188
BOWEN, Edye 37
BOXALL, Rich. 157
BOYDELL, *Ann 141; John 141*; Wm. 55
BRAY, goodwife 70
BREWER, Parnell 153; Thos. 151
BRIAN (BRYAN), Humph. 92, 183;
    Margt. 83
BRIER, Rog. 106
BROCK(E), Jeffery 135; John 135; Robt. 135
BROOKE, Thos. 89, 92
BROWN(E), Ag. 115; Ann 183; John 115;
    Rich. 131; Rog. 107
BROWNINGE, Alice 119
BRYANT, boy 3
BRYTAINE, Thos. 8
BUCKE, Christian 36; Edith 36; Gillian 36;
    Rich. 36, 131
BUFFORD(E), [blank] 59; Margt. 183
BURGENDE, Mich. 107
BURGES *(BURGIS)*, Alice 85; Ann 86;
    Joan 85, 86; John 85, *86*; Margt. 86;
    Prudence 86; Rich. 86; Robt. 85;
    Sampson 86; Ursula 85
BUR(R)NELL, John 46, 64
BURNETT *(BURNARD)*, Joan 87; *Margt.
    87*; Wm. 87
BURTTE *(BIRTE)*, Eliz. 154; *Joan 154*;
    Lettis 154; Wm. 154; *Wm. (sen.) 154*
BUS(S)HE, David 179; Elnr. 142; Humph.
    187; *John 57, 136*; Margy. 136; Mary
    136; Thos. 136
BUSHER, Alice 40; Margt. 118; Robt. 144,
    145
BUTCHER (BUCHER), [blank] 67; Ann
    72, 164; John 24, 72
BUTLER(E), Ann 109; John 11, 127;
    Margt. 109; Wm. 109
BYDE, Robt. 133
BYN, John 35
BYNYON, Adam 131
BYRDE (BIRDE) Jane 137; John 137, 183;
    Kath. 137; Mary 137; Robt. 137; Ursula
    137; Wm. 64, *137*
BYSE, Thos. 92

CABBE, Rich. 106
CABLE, Math. 57, 144

DERE, Rog. 7
DEVEROUX, Chris. 3
DEYOS (DAIES; DYEOS), Alice 155;
    Ann 155; Eliz. 155; Joyce 155;
    Nich. 155; Wm. 73, 155; Wm. (jun.)
    155
DIDMUSTER, Johane 55
DITHERIDG, Alice 45
DITTIE (DITTYE), Alice *138*, 175; Anth.
    138; *Hen. 138*; John 138; Margt. 138;
    Rich. 138
DIXON, Ann 155; Thos. 155
DOBBES, Rich. 9
DOLE, Eliz. 3; Eliz. (jun.) 3; Joan 3, 61;
    Ralph 3; Rich. 61; Thos. 3, 61; Wm. 3;
    Wm. (jun.) 61; Wm. (sen.) 61
DOLLYN, Gillian 181; Thos. 181
DOSELL, Guy 111
DOWDIN, Thos. 106
DOWER, Robt. 59, 60
DOWLE, John 59
DOWNE, Christian 58
DO(W)NINGE, Phil. 134; Wm. 192
DOWRAGE, Wm. 161
DOWTINGE, Phil. 137
DREWET, Hen. 152
DUDGIN, Margt. 119
DUKES, Eliz. 82
DURBAN, Edith 188; Robt. 188
DURAND (DURANT), Mr. 68; Ann 113;
    Morris 113
DURNELL (DORNELL), Ambrose 182;
    Eliz. 135; John 57
DYER, Rich. 68

EASON, Robt. 179
EATON, [blank] 73; John 187
EDDYE (EADDY), John 32; 165
EDWARD(E)S, goodwife 62; Alice, 11;
    Denise 89; *Edith 89*; Edm. 89; Jane 11;
    Sampson 89, 107, 122; Wm. 11, 87;
    Wm. (jun.) 11
EDWIN, Wm. 41
EERLE, Thos. 99
ELLIOT(T) (ELIOTT; ELLETT), Andr.
    167; Anth. 167; Christian 36; Dor. 36;
    Edw. 36; Harry 115; Priscilla 131;
    Thos. 131; Wm. 36
EL(L)IS, Humph. 127, 146; John 1; Margt.
    127
ELONDE, John 36; Thos. 36
ELSON, Robt. 63
ESTOPE als. White, Robt. 68
EVAN, Burnam 188; Griffin 152; Phil.
    101
EVENET, Edw. 47
EVERETTE, John 76
EWEN, Thos. 153
EYDON, Wm. 187

FAGOTT, Joan 61, Thos. 61
FARLEY, Jas. 65
FAWKETT, Thos. 133
FAWKNER, John 187
FECHETT, Rich. 1
FES(S)AUNT (PHEASANT), Ann 45;
    John 45; Kath. 45
FIAN, Dennys 10; Jane 10 see also VYAN
FIDO, Thos. 46
FIELD (FYLD), John 37
FILL, John 99
FINE (FYNN), John 40, 185
FLEETE, Wm. 125
FLEMYNGE, Ag. 156; Andr. 156; Ann
    156; Geo. 156; Joan 156; Thos. 156;
    Wm. 156
FLETCHER, Dr. 90; Eliz. 90; John 90;
    Mary 90; Nath. 90; Phoebe 90; Priscilla
    90; *Rich. 1*; Sara 90; Theo. 90
FLOWER, Alice 61; Robt. 74
FLOYD, goodman 185; Thos. 124
FOLLEN, PETER 101
FORD, Ag. 114; Francis 114; Helen 37;
    Ralph 114; Rich. 114; Susan 114
FORREST, John 120
FOSTER, Hen. 30
FOWNES (FOWENS), Joan 54; John 54
FOX, Mr. 107
FREELYNGE *(FRELING)*, Ann 38;
    Cornelius 38; Paul 38; Thos. 38
FRENCH, Ann 71; Edw. 71
FRENDE (FRIND(E); FRYNDE), Anth.
    30, 63; John 30
FREWELL, Edith 62; Robt. 62
FRYER (FRIER), Joan 141, Robt. 122;
    Walt. 141
FYANNE als. COMPANE, see COM-
    PANE als. FYANNE; see also FIAN,
    VYAN

GAINSFORT, Edw. 161
Galloway, Chris. 85
GARDNER, Rich. 30
GARLAND(E), Francis 38; Pascal 140
GARRETT *(GERRATT)*, Ag. 91; Alice 91;
    Eliz. 91; *Margt. 91*; Robt. 91
GAY, Rich. 116
GAYGE, Sam. 132
GEBEBE, Thos. 76
GEORGE (GORGE), Mr. 63; Julian 70;
    Rich. 126
GERINGE, Thos. 140
GIBBES, Wm. 183
GIBBON, Wm. 173
GIBSON, Mrs. 173; John 173; John (jun.)
    173; John (sen.) 173; Mary 173; Thos.
    (jun.) 173; Thos. (sen.) 173; Wm. 173
GILL (GYLL), John 130; 139; Robin 130;
    Wm. 130

LYLLIEWHITE (LYLLYWHITE), Eliz. 37

LYPETT, Walt. 38

M—W, Peter 61
MACEY, John 73
MACHIN (MACHAM), Benedict 54, 158
MAISY, Alice 67
MAN, John 37
MANFEELD, Rich. 172; Wm. 172
MANNINGE, Ann 100; Rich. 100
MARSHE, Ann 164
MARTIN(E) (MARTEN; MARTYN), [blank] 175; Mr. 68, 166; sister 145; Ag. 120; Joan 164; Margy. 105; Mary 105, 132; Rich. 25, 58, 88, 89, 103, 120, 128, 133, 134, 137, 158, 164, 175
MARWELL, Hen. 17; *Margt. 91; Rog. 91*
MASON(E) (MASSON), Ag. 121, *122*; Edith 178; Joan 178; John 178; Mary 178; Susan 178; Thos. 45, 121, 122
MASTERS, John 185
MATTHEWES, goodwife 166
MAY*(E)*, Harry 8; *Hen. 8*; Kath. 8
MAYNARD, Wm. 151
MAYNE, Eliz. (jun. and sen.) 179; Rich. 179; Sim. 179
MELINE (MELLEN; MELYN(E)), Morgan 190; Thos. 144; Wm. 113
MELTON [blank] 147
MEREDITHE, Owen 128
MERICK(E) (MERITH), *Ann 125*; John *125*, 190; Thos. 190
MINERER, Thos. 127
MOCKETT, Oliver 63
MODY, John 92
MOLLINOR, Rich. 6
MOMFORD, Geo. 61
MONYE, Joan 113
MOOLLYNS, John 28
MOORE (MORE), Francis 97; John 6, 97; Margt. 148; Math. 148; Rich. 97, 140; Wm. 109
MORGAN(N), Alice 84; Ann 144; Avis 26; Evan 57; Wm. 44, 88, 107
NORMAN, Anth. 35
MORRICE *(MORRES)*, *Ann 141*; Joan 141; John 141; Nich. 141
MORSE, *Agatha 191; Ag. 191*; Eliz. 60; Ellen 191; Haggas 191; Rich. 191
MOUNTAIN(E) (MONTAINE; MOWN-TAYN(E)), Arthur 131; Eliz. 106, 107; Isabel 131; Rich. 106, 107
MOWREY *(MORRYE; MORY)*, Eliz. 69; *John 69; Margt. 69*; Thos. 69
MURDOCK, Gillian 118
MURSELEY (MURSEY), Robt. 35, 192
MYDDLETON, Thos. 187

MYLLES, Chris. 94; *Edw. 142; Margy. 142*
MYLLNER, Geo. 53
MYNYFE, John (jun. and sen.) 119

NASHE, [blank] 103
NAYLER *(NAILOR)*, *Alice 70*; Ann 70; Cic. 70; *Edw. 70, 154*
NEALE (NEYLE), aunt 145; Ellen 192
NEATHWAYE, John 179
NEDE, Alice 79, 163; Math. 79, 163
NESSON(S), goodwife 107; Jonas 107
NEWES, Reginald 111
NEWMAN, Alice 18; Edw. 18; Rich. 18; Ursula 18
NEWTON(N) *(NUTON)*, Mr. 141; *David 123*; Jas. 41, 123; Joan 123; Thos. 59, 95, 118, 170, 174; Wm. 123
NICHOLAS, Ag. 142; Joan 142; *Margy. 142*; Thos. 142; Wm. 142
NICHOLLS, Ag. 71; Edw. 71; Edw. (jun.) 71; Eliz. 71; Kath. 71; Rich. 71; Thos. 71; Walt. 71
NICHOLSON, Eliz. 123; Robt. 123
NOBLE, Gilbert 185; Grace 175
NORTHALL, Eliz. 19; *John 19*; Roland 19; Susan 84
NORTHBRO(O)KE, John 9, 19
NOTTINGEGAME, John 140
NOWNE, John 179

O'DRISCOLL, Sir Finen, 31
OFFLEY, Wm. 131, 181
OLFYLDE, John 72; Mary 72
ORCHARD, John 99
OTEL(E)Y, [blank] 147; Barnard 118
OWEN, Jas. 32; John 66; Thos. 9, 21

PACKER, Ag. 124; Ralph 104; Thos. 14, 104, 124, 131, 170; Wm. 89, 124
PAGE, Rich. 131
PAINE, Mrs. 187; *John 32; Thos. 32*
PALMER, Edith 84; Eliz. 84; Jas. 84; Rich. 84
PANTER, Gabriel 185
PANTHUR(E) *(PANTER)*, Arthur 31, 82, 125; Arthur (jun.) 125; Ann 125; Fortune 125; John 125; Margt. 125; Wm. 125
PANTINGE, Hen. 175
PAR(C)KER, Eliz. 61; Robt. 145; Thos. 59, 61
PARSIVALL, John 189
PARSON(S), Mr. 119; Eliz. 82; Robt. 59
PARTHOP, John 156
PASH, Gregory 107
PATCHE, Andr. 164; Ann 164; Mary 164
PAVY, Eliz. 183
PAYTON, Alice 106; Susan 106

PEEK(E), Rich. 107
PERKIN, Joan 88; Thos. 88
PESTONE, Robt. 16
PETER, Garret 38
PETERSON, Geo. 92
PETTINGALE, Rich. 68
PHELP(E)S, Edw. 96; Thos. 65, 98; Wm. 96
PHEASANT see FESAUNT
PHILLIP(P)S (PHYLLIPS), Joan 70; John
    47; Thos. 107
PICKERELL, Ellen 132
PILL, Wm. 142
PINCHIN (PYNCHYN), Thos. 1, 189
PINCKE, Clement 107
PITCHER, Mr. 185; Mrs. 145
PITT, Thos. 184
PITTES (PYTTES), Alice 160; John 73,
    160; John (jun.) 160; *Margt. 160*; Mary
    160; Maud 3; Rich. 3; *53*; Thos. 160;
    Wm. 53
PLACER, Arthur 145
PLEVIE, Joan 119
PLOVER, Susan 130
POLLINGTON, Eliz. 84
POOLE, Anne 104
POORE, Ag. 131
POPAM, Frances 183
POPE, Elnr. 143; Eliz. 143; Giles 143; John
    85; Robt. 143; Thos. 143; Wm. 143
POPLEY, Ann 73; Derrick 73; Edm. 73;
    Edm. (jun.) 73; Joan 73; *John 73*
PORTER, Arthur 187
POURNELL, John 154
POWELL, Auberry/*Alborowe* 74; Ann 180;
    Chris. 6; *Edw. 8*; Eliz. 56; John 33, 74;
    Kath. 8; Walt. 74
POWNOLL, aunt 90; Mr. 90; Nath. 90
POYNER *(POYNARD)*, *Barth. 144*;
    Clemence/*Clementine* 144
PRESTWOD, Thos. 67
PREWETT, mistress 67; Anth. 145; Joan
    145; Wm. 145
PRICE, Francis 159; Margt. 166; Thos. 166
PRICHARD, Lewis 57
PRIDDIE, Wm. 85
PRIN (PRYN), Mr. 50; Edw. 1; Margt. 1;
    Thos. 24, 57, 64, 155
PROSSER als. PRORSER, Kath. 180;
    Rich. 180
PRYER, Thos. 64
PUNCHARD, Peter 81
PUX(S)TON, Alice 155; Thos. 87, 155
PYCKTHORNE, Mich. 136
PYLL, John 188
PYLLYNG, Elnr. 97; Rich. 97
PYMASE, Ellen 192

RAWLIN(G)S *(RAWLEINS)*, Joan *21*, 168;
    Thos. 21; Wm. 8

RAYE, Anth. 82
READ(E), goodwife 10; Mr. 183; Jane 61;
    John 35, 106; John (jun.) 35; Peter 61;
    Rich. 103; Thos. 153
READINGE, Hugh 161; Margt. 161
REDWOOD, Rich. 105; Robt. 160, 172
REGERES see ROGERS
RESTALL, John 190
RICARTE, Arth. 22
RICHARDES, Maud 131
RICHMANN, Eliz. 171; John 171
RICHMOND, John 85
RID(D)ER (RYDER(E)), Alice 23, 75;
    John 191; Thos. 23, 75; Wm. 75
RIDLER, Rich. 145
RISBY, Chris. 46; Dor. 46; *Joan 46; Maur.
    46*; Nich. 46; Robt. 46; Thos. 46; *Wm.
    46*
RISSE (RYSE), [blank] 192; Peter 160
ROAN(ES), Joan 3; Susan 3; Wm. 3
ROBERTES, Alice 168; *Edm. 88; Edw. 52*;
    Hen. 55; *Joan 88*
ROBINS (ROBYNS), Amy 47; *Ann 47*;
    John 1; Nich. 47
ROBINSON, [blank] 73; Wm. 68, 69, 73,
    96, 117, 153, 165, 168, 173
ROCKWELL, goodman 37
ROE, John 35; Peter 183
ROGERS (REGER(E)S), Mrs. 150; Edw.
    76; Eliz. 48, 66; *Elnr. 150*; Jas. 35; Jane
    164; John 76; *Rich. 48, 150*; Robt. 150;
    Thos. 48, 76; Welsyon 76
ROOME, Edw. 60; John 60
ROTHE, Eliz. 26
ROTHELL als. ROTHWELL, Alice 126;
    Eliz. 126; John 126; Nich. 126; Rich.
    126; Walt. 126
RUDGE, Eliz. 185
RUNWAY, Lewis 101
RYHMAN, [blank] 140

S—, Joan 103
SALISBURY, [blank] 185
SAMU—, Mr. 152
SANFFLOCKE, John 89
*SARCHES, Alborowe/Alb(r)o(u)gh/Albero
    74; Rich. 74*
SAUNDERS (SAWNDERS), Ag. 2; Eliz.
    2; John 2, 101; John (jun.) 101; Wm.
    101 see also JELLIS als. SAUNDERS
SAYER, J. 89
SCAMP(E), Ann 172; John 172; John (jun.)
    172; Susan 172
SCULLICK (SCOLICK), Eliz. 49; Maud
    49
SESSELL see CECILL
SETTLE (SETTELL), John 63, 102; *Kath.
    102*, Margt. 102; *Maud/Matilda/
    Magdalen 102*; Thos. 102

INDEX OF PLACES

INDEX OF SUBJECTS